Up & Running
with Flight Simulator

Up & Running
with Flight Simulator®

Frank Dille
Frank Raudszus
Nick Dargahi

San Francisco • Paris • Düsseldorf • Soest

Acquisitions Editor: Dianne King
Series Editor: Joanne Cuthbertson
Translator: John Cantrell, Tristan Translations
Editor: Judith Ziajka
Technical Editor: Nick Dargahi
Word Processors: Paul Erickson, Lisa Mitchell
Book Designer: Elke Hermanowski
Icon Designer: Helen Bruno
Technical Art: Delia Brown
Screen Graphics: Delia Brown, Cuong Le
Desktop Production Artist: Helen Bruno
Proofreader: Barbara Dahl
Indexer: Ted Laux
Cover Designer: Archer Designs

Figures 14.1 and 15.3 ©1983-1989 Microsoft Corporation. Reproduced with permission of Microsoft.

Microsoft is a registered trademark of Microsoft Corporation.

Flight Simulator is a registered trademark of SubLOGIC Corporation.

SYBEX is a registered trademark of SYBEX Inc.

TRADEMARKS: SYBEX has attempted throughout this book to distinguish proprietary trademarks from descriptive terms by following the capitalization style used by the manufacturer.

SYBEX is not affiliated with any manufacturer.

Every effort has been made to supply complete and accurate information. However, SYBEX assumes no responsibility for its use, nor for any infringement of the intellectual property rights of third parties which would result from such use.

Library of Congress Card Number: 90-71027
ISBN: 0-89588-738-X

Manufactured in the United States of America
10 9 8 7

Up & Running

Let's say that you are comfortable with your PC. You know the basic functions of word processing, spreadsheets, and database management. In short, you are a committed and eager PC user who would like to gain familiarity with several popular programs as quickly as possible. The Up & Running series of books from SYBEX has been developed for you.

Who this book is for

This clearly structured guide shows you in 20 steps what the product can do, how you make it work, and how soon you can achieve practical results.

What this book provides

Your Up & Running book thus satisfies two needs: It describes the program's capabilities, and it lets you quickly get acquainted with the program's operation. This provides valuable help for a purchase decision, along with a 20-step basic course that will give you a solid foundation in the program—even if you're a beginner with scant prior knowledge.

The benefits are plain to see. First, you invest in software that meets your needs because, thanks to the appropriate Up & Running book, you will know the program's features and limitations. Second, once you purchase the product, you can skip the instruction manual and learn the basics of the program by following the 20 steps.

We have structured the Up & Running books so that the busy user spends little time studying documentation and so that the beginner is not burdened with unnecessary text.

Structure of the book

A clock shows your work time for each step. This indicates how much time you can expect to spend on each step with your computer.

Required time

45

Clock

Naturally, you'll need much less time if you only read through the steps rather than carrying them out at your computer. You can also save some time by scanning the short notes in the margins to find the most important sections within a step.

Three symbols are used to highlight points of special note. These symbols and their meanings are shown below:

Symbols

Action

Tip

Warning

An Up & Running book cannot, of course, replace a book or manual containing advanced applications. However, you will get the information needed to put the program to practical use and to learn its basic functions.

The first step always covers software installation in relation to hardware requirements. You'll learn how to operate the program with your available hardware. Various methods for starting the program are also explained.

The remaining 19 steps demonstrate basic functions, using examples or short descriptions. The last steps cover special program features. If information regarding recently announced program versions is available at printing time, new features are introduced to the extent possible.

Now you see how an Up & Running book will save you time and money.

SYBEX is very interested in your reaction to the Up & Running series. Your opinions and suggestions help all readers, and thereby help you.

Preface

With Microsoft® Flight Simulator® 4.0, armchair pilots everywhere can experience the thrill of flying with greater realism than ever before. This fourth-generation real-time flight simulator offers several new improvements over its predecessor version 3.0. These include custom 80386 modules to make the program run faster on 386 machines, improved flight handling characteristics, dynamic scenery such as other aircraft and ground traffic, experimental aircraft you can design yourself, a sailplane, random weather variations, more realistic runway approach lighting systems, and air traffic control communications.

The sophistication and verisimilitude of Flight Simulator 4.0 quickly dispel any notions that this program is just a "game." In the U.S., for example, the new version is used to train private pilots.

This Up & Running book introduces you to Flight Simulator in 20 fast and easy steps. From your first takeoff to a barnstorming tour of the San Francisco Bay Area, you will become familiar with the complex array of instruments, controls and navigational aids. Welcome to the world of virtual reality.

Nick Dargahi
San Francisco, July 1990

Table of Contents

Step 1

Installation

Before your first flight with the Cessna Skylane RG II or the Gates Learjet 25G on Flight Simulator, you must customize the program to your hardware and install it on your hard disk, if you are using one. Step 1 describes this simple, easy-to-perform installation and configuration.

System Requirements

The high-performance Flight Simulator 4.0 from Microsoft requires the following minimum configuration:

- An IBM PC, XT, AT, or PS/2, or a compatible computer
- At least 384 KB of RAM
- One floppy disk drive
- MS-DOS or PC-DOS, version 2.0 or later
- CGA, EGA, VGA, PS/2 Graphics System, or Hercules monochrome or Incolor card
- Appropriate monitor for your graphics adapter card

You can load the program more quickly and easily if you use a hard disk. The following additional peripheral devices also are useful:

- A mouse
- One or two joysticks
- A modem
- Navigational maps, available from Microsoft (without these maps, you will not be able to navigate your plane between cities, nor will you be able to fly effectively under instrument flying conditions, because VOR radio beacons are not listed in the Microsoft manual)

Preparing Your Disks

*Making
backup
copies*

Before you install or start the program, be sure to make backup copies of the original floppy disks. Microsoft does not use copy protection, so backing up the floppy disks for personal use is simple.

Put the original floppy disk in drive A and enter the command **DISKCOPY A: A:**. Then follow the screen instructions. As soon as you have copied a disk, attach an appropriately prepared label to the target disk.

If you have two floppy disk drives, put the first original floppy disk in drive A and a blank target disk in drive B. Copy the original disk by entering the MS-DOS command **DISKCOPY A: B:**. Repeat the copying operation with the scenery floppy disk.

Starting from the Program Floppy Disk

You can start Flight Simulator directly from the program floppy disk with the command **FS**. The configuration menu appears. Start customizing the program to your hardware.

Installing the Program on a Hard Disk

You can also install the program in a subdirectory on the hard disk. First create a new subdirectory on the hard disk.

Go to the desired hard disk or hard disk partition and enter the command **MD FS4**. Then move into this subdirectory by entering **CD FS4**. Put the program floppy disk in drive A and start copying with the command **COPY A:*.***. Then switch the program floppy disk for the scenery disk and repeat the copying procedure.

Configuring Your Program

Before starting Flight Simulator, you must customize the program for your hardware. Activate the configuration menu by entering **FS**.

You need to configure your Flight Simulator program only once. The AUTOEXEC.FS4 file stores this data. You access this previous definition when you start the program by entering **FS4**. The configuration data in this file lets you easily start Flight Simulator the next time you want to run the program.

Specifying the Start Option

When the first menu appears on the screen, select option 1, Go through Startup Menu. Move through the submenus for this option to customize your program. Figure 1.1 shows the Startup menu.

By selecting option 2, No-Questions-Asked Startup, you achieve the same effect as when you enter FS4, described in the preceding section. When you select option 2, you move directly to the starting mode of the program. You find yourself in the cockpit of the Cessna on the runway of Meigs Field in Chicago (you can modify the program to start at a different location and in a different mode, if you prefer).

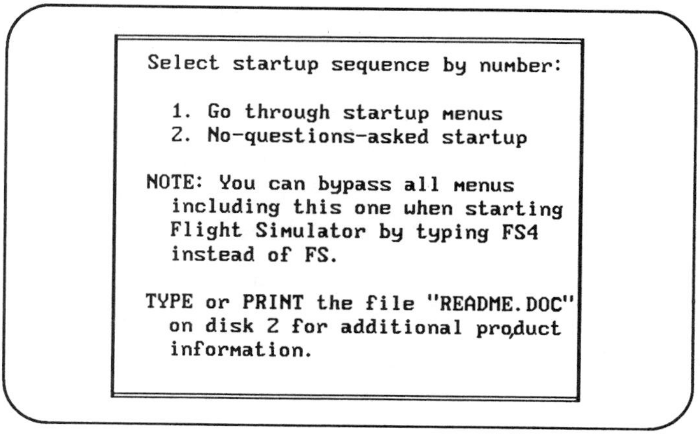

Going directly to the starting mode

```
Select startup sequence by number:

   1. Go through startup menus
   2. No-questions-asked startup

NOTE: You can bypass all menus
   including this one when starting
   Flight Simulator by typing FS4
   instead of FS.

TYPE or PRINT the file "README.DOC"
   on disk 2 for additional product
   information.
```

Figure 1.1: Startup menu

Specifying Processor Drivers

For the processor driver, enter the processor used by your computer. Owners of a 386-type system can select a 32-bit driver to improve screen drawing. If you are using a PC or XT or compatible computer, press A. If you are using an AT or other 80286-based system, press B. If you are using an 80386-based system, press C.

Specifying the Video Adapter

Flight Simulator supports Hercules monochrome or InColor cards and CGA cards plus all the conventional EGA cards and high-resolution VGA cards. Specify the one your system uses. Figure 1.2 shows the video adapter selection screen.

```
What display are you using?

A. Color composite monitor (CGA)
B. Black and white monitor (CGA)
C. RGB monitor (CGA)
D. Liquid crystal display (CGA)
E. Hercules monochrome or Blue Chip
F. EGA monochrome
G. EGA 16 color 320x200 RGB mon
H. EGA 16 color 640x350 ENHANCED mon
I. IBM PS/2 16 color 320x200
J. IBM PS/2 256 color 320x200
K. Hercules InColor 16 color 720x348
L. Tandy 1000 16 color 320x200
M. VGA 16 color 640x350 ENHANCED mon

(Press a letter: A,B,C, etc.)
```

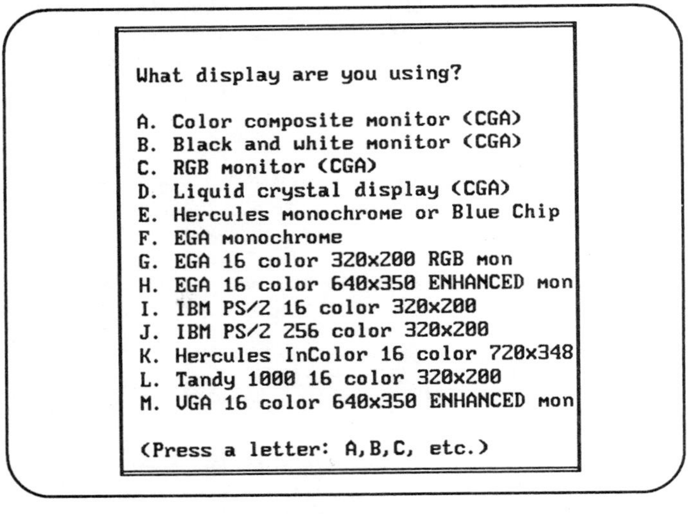

Figure 1.2: Video adapter selection screen

Specifying the Operating Mode

Selecting a demonstration flight

From the next menu you select the operating mode. You can select a demonstration flight by choosing option C or D (without sound). Select option A to start in normal flight mode. Select Option B to have the program use the system date and time. Figure 1.3 shows the operating mode selection screen.

Specifying Environment Conditions

You can load the random weather generator or dynamic scenery, or both, as early as the installation. Owners of a slow PC or XT-type computer, however, should do without these two features, to increase the resolution. Figure 1.4 shows the environment conditions selection screen.

Specifying the Keyboard

You control Flight Simulator mainly with the keyboard. In the next menu, you need to tell the program which keyboard you are using and where the function keys are located.

Specifying a Logbook

In the next menu item, you can specify whether you want to keep a logbook and, if you do, the name under which it is to be stored. If you press Y for Yes, a box appears asking you to enter the logbook name ID. Type a name and press the Enter key.

```
Select operating mode:

A. Normal flight mode
B. Normal flight using system
   date & time
C. Demo mode
D. Demo without sound

(Press A,B,C, or D)
```

Figure 1.3: Operating mode selection screen

```
Select Environment Conditions:

A. Use dynamic scenery
B. Use random weather
C. Both
D. Neither (highest display rate)

(Press A,B,C, or D)
```

Figure 1.4: Environment conditions selection screen

Specifying User Interfaces

When you use joysticks, the mouse yoke controls are overridden. You can still use the mouse pointer to pull down menus and activate selected controls, but you cannot use the mouse to steer your plane.

To use a mouse or one or more joysticks, press Y for Yes in the menu boxes that appear on the screen.

Using a mouse

If you want to control the program with a mouse, an appropriate mouse driver must be installed in your system. For the Microsoft Mouse, use a mouse driver program called MOUSE.COM that is run by your AUTO-EXEC.BAT batch file when you boot your computer, or use a mouse driver file called MOUSE.SYS that is declared in your CONFIG.SYS file.

Using joysticks

When you use joysticks to control your plane, you must specify what part of the plane each joystick controls. Flight Simulator 4.0 allows you to select one joystick to control the yoke of your plane and another, optional joystick to control either the throttles and brake or the throttles and rudder. Choose the setup you prefer on the joystick parameters specification screen, shown in Figure 1.5. If you are using only one joystick, select option A.

```
      JOYSTICK SELECTION OPTION

  A. Stick A - Yoke

  B. Stick A - Yoke
     Stick B - Throttle/Brakes

  C. Stick A - Yoke
     Stick B - Throttle/Rudder

  (Press A,B, or C to select.)
```

Figure 1.5: Joystick parameters specification screen

After you specify the joystick parameters, the program asks you to place your joystick in a position that the program can calibrate for its initial settings. Center your joystick. Then press any key to continue.

Step 2

The Keyboard

This step introduces the basic operation of Flight Simulator. In particular, you will learn the keys and key combinations and their functions.

In addition to controlling the program with a mouse, a joystick, or the cursor keys, you can also manipulate aircraft controls and slewing movement with the function keys. The placement of some function keys depends on the type of keyboard you are using.

Controlling your air-craft with function keys

Function Keys on Enhanced Keyboards

If you are using an enhanced keyboard, the keys in the top row of the keyboard perform the operations listed in Table 2.1. Figure 2.1 shows these keys.

Function keys in the top row of the key-board

Key	Function
F1	Cut the engine.
F2	Reduce throttle.
F3	Increase throttle.
F4	Use full throttle.
F5	Set flaps up.
F6	Set flaps to 10°.
F7	Set flaps to 30°.
F8	Set flaps down.

Table 2.1: Function Keys on the Top Row of the Keyboard

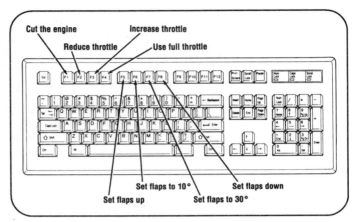

Figure 2.1: Function keys on the top row of the keyboard

Function Keys on Standard Keyboards

Function keys at the left side of the keyboard

If you are using a standard keyboard, the keys at the left side of the keyboard perform the operations listed in Table 2.2. Figure 2.2 shows these keys.

Key	Function
F1	Set flaps up.
F2	Use full throttle.
F3	Set flaps to 10°.
F4	Increase throttle two steps.
F5	Set flaps to 20°.
F6	Increase throttle one step.
F7	Set flaps to 30°.
F8	Reduce throttle.
F9	Set flaps down.
F10	Cut the engine.

Table 2.2: Function Keys on the Left Side of the Keyboard

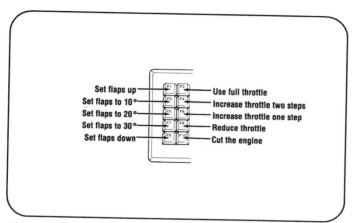

Figure 2.2: Function keys on the left side of the keyboard

Function Keys on the Main Keypad

Table 2.3 lists the keys on the main keypad that control Flight Simulator functions. Figure 2.3 shows these keys.

Key	Function
A	Calibrate altimeter.
B	Toggle DME between Nav 1 and Nav 2 radios.
C	Tune Com radio.
D	Calibrate gyroscope.
F	Toggle DME speed to station or distance.
G	Set landing gear up or down.
H	Turn carburetor heat on or off.
I	Turn smoke or spray on or off.
K	Calibrate joystick.

Table 2.3: Function Keys on the Main Keypad

Key	Function
L	Turn lights on or off.
M	Display magneto menu.
N	Tune Nav radios.
O	Turn strobes on or off.
P	Pause.
Q	Turn sound on or off.
S	Change view out selected 3-D window.
T	Select transponder squawk code.
V	Choose OBI heading for selected VOR station.
Z	Activate autopilot.
Backspace	Restore 1 × Zoom.
Esc	Turn menu bar on or off. Also used to exit a pull-down menu or menu dialog box.
Num Lock	Activate map window.
Prt Scr	Reset flight mode.
.	Activate wheel brakes.
;	Save flight mode.
"	Make window topmost.
+	Zoom in a selected window.
−	Zoom out selected window.
[	Select or activate 3-D window 1.
]	Select or activate 3-D window 2.

Table 2.3: Function Keys on the Main Keypad (continued)

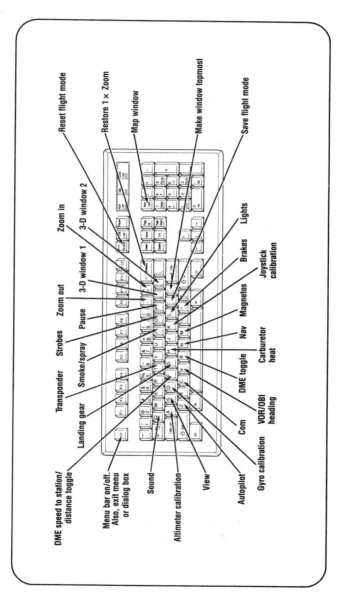

Figure 2.3: Function keys on the main keypad

Function Keys on the Numeric Keypad

Table 2.4 lists the keys on the numeric keypad that control Flight Simulator operations. Figure 2.4 shows these keys.

Key	Function
1	Set elevator trim up.
2	Pitch nose up.
3	Reduce throttle.
4	Set left ailerons.
5	Set center ailerons.
6	Set right ailerons.
7	Set elevator trim down.
8	Pitch nose down.
9	Increase throttle.
0	Turn rudder left.
Bottom-right key	Turn rudder right.

(The bottom-right key is the key at the bottom right of the keypad.)

Table 2.4: Function Keys on the Numeric Keypad

Navigation Communication Keys

Certain keys or key combinations control navigation and communication functions, as shown in Table 2.5.

Key/Combination	Function
B	Control DME toggle for Nav 1/Nav 2 radios.
C +	Set the integer Com frequency.

Table 2.5: Navigation and Communication keys

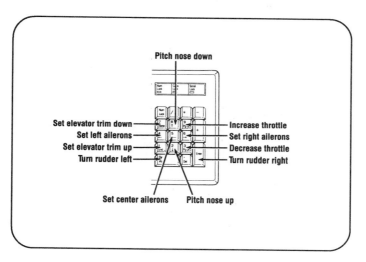

Figure 2.4: Function keys on the numeric keypad

Key/Combination	Function
C C +	Set the fractional Com frequency.
F	Control DME display toggle for distance or speed to a VOR station.
N 1 +	Set the integer Nav 1.
N N 1 +	Set the fractional Nav 1.
N 2 +	Set the integer Nav 2.
N N 2 +	Set the fractional Nav 2.
T +	Set the first digit of the transponder frequency.
T T +	Set the second digit of the transponder frequency.
T T T +	Set the third digit of the transponder frequency.

Table 2.5: Navigation and Communication keys (continued)

Key/Combination	Function
T T T T +	Set the fourth digit of the transponder frequency.
V 1 +	Control top OBI course selector.
V 2 +	Control bottom OBI course selector.
Z	Control autopilot toggle.

Table 2.5: Navigation and Communication keys (continued)

In addition to using the + (plus) key to increase numerical values, you can use the - (minus) key to decrease numerical values. (Note that the plus key referred to in Table 2.5 is the plus key on the main keypad, not the one on the numeric keypad.)

View Keys

Certain keys or key combinations control view functions, as shown in Table 2.6.

Key/Combination	Function
Scroll Lock 1...9	Select view direction.
[	Turn on 3-D window 1.
[[	Turn off 3-D window 1.
]	Turn on 3-D window 2.
]]	Turn off 3-D window 2.
NumLock	Turn on the map window.
NumLock NumLock	Turn off the map window.
S	Select the view.
+	Zoom in on the current window.
-	Zoom out.

Table 2.6: View Keys

Key/Combination	Function
Backspace	Restore Zoom to magnification factor of 1.
Shift-Enter	Pan down.
Shift-Backspace	Pan up.
``	Make this window topmost.

Table 2.6: View Keys (continued)

Slewing Controls

Slewing is a special nonflight mode that allows you to move very quickly or very slowly from point to point in the Flight Simulator world. In addition to actually moving the plane to a new location (called translation), you can reorient the plane to any attitude you wish (called rotation).

The slewing controls work only when you are in slew mode, which you enter by selecting option 9 on the Nav/Com menu.

Slewing Translation Controls

The keys listed in Table 2.7 control slewing movement.

Key	Function
2	Slew backward.
4	Slew left.
5	Freeze translation or rotation.
6	Slew right.
8	Slew forward.
A	Slew down in altitude.
Q	Slew up in altitude.

Table 2.7: Slewing Movement Keys

The numbers in Table 2.7 are the numbers on the numeric keypad.

Slewing Rotation Controls

The keys listed in Table 2.8 control slewing orientation.

Key	Function
1	Yaw left (change heading).
3	Yaw right (change heading).
5	Freeze rotation or translation.
7	Roll or bank left.
9	Roll or bank right.
9	Pitch nose up.
0	Pitch nose down.

Table 2.8: Slewing Orientation Keys

The numbers in Table 2.8 are the numbers on the numeric keypad, except for the numbers in boldface (**9** and **0**), which are numbers on the main keypad.

Other Slewing Functions

The keys listed in Table 2.9 control other slewing functions.

Key	Function
Z	Turn position display on or off.
Alt	Center plane so that it is level:
	Heading: North
	Pitch: Straight ahead
	Bank: 0°

Table 2.9: Other Slewing Function Keys

World War I Ace Function Keys

To use the World War I Ace function keys, you must be in World War I Ace flying mode. (You select this mode from the Entertainment menu, which you reach via the Mode menu.) Table 2.10 lists the keys available.

Key/Combination	Function
R	Display war report.
W	Declare war.
X	Drop bomb.
Spacebar	Fire machine guns.

Table 2.10: World War I Ace Function Keys

Mouse Controls

Tables 2.11 and 2.12 list mouse movements and their functions. Figure 2.5 illustrates mouse functions. The mouse pointer must not be visible on the screen when you perform any of the following actions (press the right mouse button to toggle the pointer on and off).

Mouse Movement	Function
Forward	Pitch nose down.
Backward	Pitch nose up.
Left	Set left aileron (bank left).
Right	Set right aileron (bank right).

Table 2.11: Mouse Controls

Mouse Movement	Function
Forward	Increase throttle.
Backward	Decrease throttle.
Left	Apply brakes.
Right	Release brakes.

Table 2.12: Mouse Controls (Left Mouse Button Pressed)

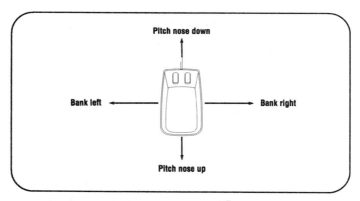

Figure 2.5: Mouse functions

The mouse can also be use in slew mode. To activate the mouse in slew mode, click the right mouse button so that the mouse pointer disappears from the screen. Then to move forward, move the mouse forward; to move backward, move the mouse backward. To rotate left or right, move the mouse left or right, but notice that you are not actually translating the plane's position (unless you are already in motion), but merely rotating in place. To stop all motion, click the left mouse button. To make the mouse pointer reappear, click the right mouse button.

Step 3

Menu 1: Mode

The Mode menu lets you select from among six operating modes. You also can select aircraft from the aircraft library or design your own plane, choose a preexisting mode or create a new mode in the flight mode library, and run a demonstration showing Flight Simulator's capabilities or record your own demonstration to be played back later. To call the Mode menu, select the Mode option on the menu bar or simply press the 1 key on the main keypad (not the 1 key on the numeric keypad). Figure 3.1 shows the Mode menu.

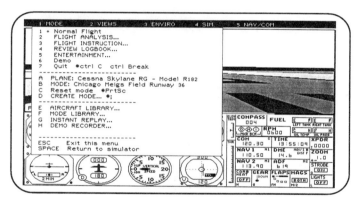

Figure 3.1: Mode menu

1: Normal Flight

When you select the Normal Flight option, the program aborts the current flight and starts the mode selected in the flight mode library. The default startup mode puts your plane on runway 36 of Meigs Field in Chicago.

2: Flight Analysis

Using the Flight Analysis option, you can improve your flying abilities by analyzing flight maneuvers afterward. Analyze maneuvers using landing, course plotting, or maneuver analysis graphs. The Flight Analysis menu (Figure 3.2) offers three options.

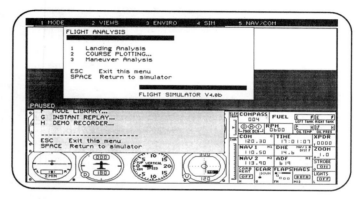

Figure 3.2: Flight Analysis menu

1: Landing Analysis

The Landing Analysis option reports the most important data related to your landing.

Start landing analysis during your landing approach at an altitude of about 200 feet.

After the airplane lands and rolls to a stop, the analysis graph appears on the screen. This graph contains information regarding your vertical speed while landing and your approach path as a function of altitude. The program automatically determines and displays the length scale.

2: Course Plotting

Using the Course Plotting option, you can record the course you flew and display it directly behind the aircraft in three dimensions in the scenery.

From the Course Plotting menu (Figure 3.3) begin recording the course by specifying option 1, Recording: On. Using option 2, specify the resolution. For short flight maneuvers, choose fine resolution. For longer flights, choose coarse resolution.

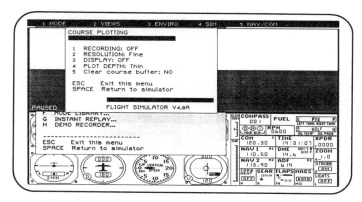

Figure 3.3: Course Plotting menu

Using option 3, you can display the course contained in the course buffer. The buffer is very small, so you may want to continuously erase the oldest course record, using option 5.

3: Maneuver Analysis

Use the Maneuver Analysis option to display the flight course. Maneuver analysis is similar to landing analysis, but course recording begins the moment you leave the Flight Analysis menu and ends when you press the \ key. The graph displayed then shows the flight path over ground.

3: Flight Instruction

The Flight Instruction option lets you choose among numerous flight practice lessons. The maneuvers covered in these lessons are ideally suited for learning the basics of flying. However, even relatively experienced pilots can obtain important information regarding extreme flight situations, navigation, and aerobatics.

*Selecting
a lesson*

After choosing option 3, Flight Instruction, select a lesson from the list on the screen. You can call up additional lessons, such as flight instructions for advanced pilots or aerobatics, by selecting option W. After you finish the exercise, various graphs help you analyze errors. Figure 3.4 shows the Flight Instruction menu.

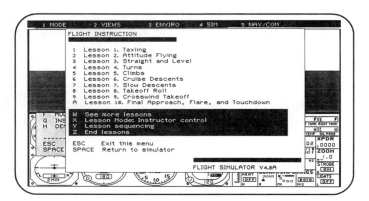

Figure 3.4: Flight Instruction menu

X: Lesson Mode: Instructor Control

Press the X key from the Flight Instruction menu box to toggle between student and instructor control. Use student control if you want to assume direct responsibility for a flight, with only the displayed flight notices for assistance. Use instructor control if you want a flight maneuver flown by an "instructor" first.

Y: Lesson Sequencing

You can immediately repeat a flight exercise by pressing the Y key for the Lesson Sequencing option when you are operating in instructor control mode. This option is a toggle.

Z: End Lesson

Press the Z key to end lesson mode and return to the Mode menu.

Ending flight instructions

4: Review Logbook

Select the Review Logbook option by choosing item 4 on the main Mode menu. Option 1 of the submenu displays the logbook and calls the logbook editor. From this editor, you can change the flight date and the remarks field. This file is stored in ASCII format, so you can edit and print the logbook using almost any word processing program.

Printing the logbook

5: Entertainment

After you have finished your first flight hours, you can use the Entertainment option to refine, in a game setting, the skills you learned. The Entertainment menu is discussed in detail later in this book. Figure 3.5 shows the Entertainment submenu. The following sections discuss its options.

1: Multi-player

You can integrate a second aircraft into your simulation by connecting to an additional computer, using the Multi-player option. With this option, data is exchanged through serial ports using a connecting cable or modem.

2: Flying in Formation

You can use the Flying in Formation option to follow an aircraft controlled by the computer. Seven different flights are available.

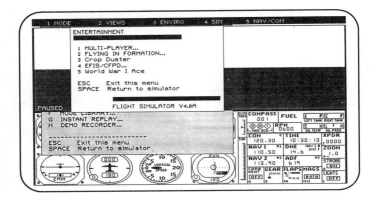

Figure 3.5: Entertainment menu

You can take off for a joint night flight over Chicago, fly through artificial walls and under bridges, or try to land on an aircraft carrier.

3: Crop Duster

The Crop Duster option activates a game in which you try to spray insecticide uniformly over a field divided into parcels. You play against the clock. The program displays your score at the end of the game.

4: EFIS/CFPD

Using front windshield projection

The electronic flight instrument systems or command flight path display (EFIS/CFPD) option lets you make an instrument landing system (ILS) landing approach with the help of computer graphics projected on the front cockpit windshield. This projection shows you the way to the airport runway as well as the proper glide slope path.

5: World War I Ace

The World War I ace option lets you go back in time to a dogfight during the First World War. Try to bomb the enemy's fuel depots and factories. To become an ace, you must shoot down five enemy fighters.

6: Demo

Use the Demonstration option to call up a demonstration flight. These demonstration sequences help acquaint you with many properties of the Flight Simulator program.

7: Quit

Select the Quit option to end Flight Simulator. You also can exit the simulator by pressing the Ctrl-C or Ctrl-Break key combinations.

A: Plane

The Plane menu option lets you specify your aircraft type. Press the A key or select this option with a mouse. Five aircraft are available for selection:

- Cessna Skylane Turbo RG II model R182

- Gates Learjet 25G

- Sopwith Camel

- Schweizer 2-32 Sailplane

- Experimental Aircraft

B: Mode

Press the B key in the main Mode menu to select the Mode option. This option gives you quick access to a limited number of flight modes. You can call up the complete list of flight situations by pressing F; this submenu displays the flight mode library. You can make selected parts of the flight mode library available as a default selection for the Mode B option. You also can integrate into the flight mode library additional modes that you have created.

C: Reset Mode

To interrupt flight in a selected mode and start with the initial mode conditions, select Reset Mode. If you are outside the main menu, you can press the PrtScr key to achieve the same results.

D: Create Mode

You can store every flight condition as a mode and incorporate it into the flight mode library. The program records all the important data regarding the simulation environment and the aircraft. To store flight information, interrupt the flight by pressing the ; key, or select the Create Mode menu option. In the submenu that appears, enter the mode title using option 1 and save the mode using option 4. The program uses the first eight letters of the specified title as the file name. To use a different file name, rename the file before saving it, using option 2. Use option 3 to store the aircraft used for the mode in the flight mode file.

E: Aircraft Library

The Aircraft Library menu option lists the aircraft types available for selection and a specification report for each type. The specification report lists the most important performance data for the aircraft type and displays a picture of the selected aircraft. If you want to delete the selected aircraft, select option 8.

F: Mode Library

Selecting a flight mode

Use the Mode Library option to display flight modes. To select previously stored flight modes, press keys 1 to 6. To display all other modes, press the 7 key. To display the mode report for the selected mode on the screen, press the 8 key. To delete a mode, press the 9 key. Figure 3.6 shows the Mode Library menu.

A: Change Selected Mode Name

Use the Change Selected Mode Name option to rename user-created modes or the file name of these selected modes.

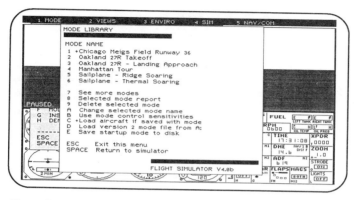

Figure 3.6: Mode Library menu

B: Use Mode Control Sensitivities

Use the Use Mode Control Sensitivities option to change the sensitivity of the joystick or mouse for a stored mode.

C: Load Aircraft If Stored with Mode

The Load Aircraft If Stored with Mode option loads the called mode with the aircraft stored in the mode data.

D: Load Version 2 Mode File from A:

The Load Version 2 Mode File from A: option lets you load old modes from Flight Simulator 2.0. To do this, insert the floppy disk containing the old flight modes in drive A and then press the D key. The program then reads the old flight types. You can rename them by using the Change Selected Mode Name option from the Mode Library screen.

You can copy and use Flight Simulator Version 3.0 modes directly into the FS 4 directory or onto the program disk without change.

E: Save Startup Mode to Disk

Use the Save Startup Mode to Disk option to specify the startup mode. This option lets you start somewhere other than Meigs Field (Chicago) runway 36. The next time you start the program, you will begin with the newly saved conditions. Mark the mode you want to use and press the E key.

G: Instant Replay

During every phase of a flight, you can interrupt the flight and display a direct replay of the last seconds.

1: Replay Seconds Set

The Replay Seconds Set option displays the number of seconds available for replay. Specify the length of the replay using option 1.

2: Auto-loop

To repeatedly replay the last phase of the flight, select the Auto-loop option. To cancel this option, press the Esc key.

3: Replay Speed in %

Use the Replay Speed in % option to specify the replay speed. You can specify the speed in the range 20 percent of actual speed (slow) to 255 percent of actual speed (fast).

H: Demo Recorder

As previously discussed, Flight Simulator provides you with demonstration flights. By selecting the Demo Recorder option, you can call the various demonstrations individually, store a demonstration as a startup demonstration, or record your own demonstrations.

1 to 5: Recordings

Items 1 to 5 on the Demo Recorder Menu list the available demonstrations.

Specify a demonstration from this list, or list other choices using item 6.

Selecting a demonstration

6: See More Demos

To call additional demonstration files, use the See More Demos option.

7: Begin Demo Recording

Select Begin Demo Recording to start recording a flight as a demonstration. To start recording, choose Begin Demo Recording and press the Esc key or the spacebar.

Note that demonstration recording accepts input only from the keyboard. It does not register or store joystick or mouse input.

8: Stop Demo Recording

To stop the demonstration recording started with the Begin Demo Recording option, press the \ key or select the Stop Demo Recording option. In a window, the program prompts you to specify whether to record the demonstration on a floppy disk or a hard disk. Specify the name of the file where the demonstration is to be stored.

9: Delete Demo

After you select and mark a demonstration, you can use the Delete Demo Option to delete it. Use this option with care because it permanently deletes selected demonstrations that you create. It does not, however, delete the prerecorded demos that came with Flight Simulator.

A: Change Demo Name

To rename a demonstration file, choose the Change Demo Name option.

B: Demo Loop

Select the Demo Loop option to repeat a demonstration again and again.

You can end the demonstration replay, or any demonstration, by pressing the Esc key. A dialog box will tell you that the demonstration is finished and ask you to again press the Esc key and then the P key to resume normal flying.

C: Save Startup Demo

Defining a startup demonstration

Choose the Save Startup Demo option to define a selected demonstration as a startup demonstration.

D: Recording Interval

Use the Recording Interval option to change the recording interval. During recording, you can press the 6 key on the main keypad to change the interval to 1 second and the 7 key on the main keypad to change the interval to 5 seconds.

I: Aircraft Design

Among the most interesting innovations in version 4.0 of Flight Simulator is the feature that lets you design and construct your own aircraft. To use the Aircraft Design option, first select Experimental Aircraft from the Plane option menu. At this point, the additional menu option I, Aircraft Design, appears in the Mode pull-down menu. After you select option I, a submenu appears in which you can vary virtually all important aircraft parameters. Make only small enhancements to the basic models provided or explore the limits of aircraft construction. However, not all designs will be able to lift off from the runway or achieve stable flight. In such a case, the program prompts you to return to the drawing board and construct a powerful, flight-capable aircraft by making new changes. Figure 3.7 shows the Aircraft Design menu.

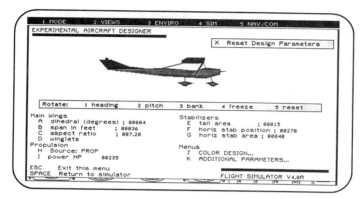

Figure 3.7: Aircraft Design menu

H–I: Propulsion

First, select the the type of plane for your design using the Source Option (item H). Three aircraft models are available:

Selecting the aircraft type

- Schweizer 2-32 (sailplane)
- Cessna Skylane RG Model 182 (propeller airplane)
- Northrop F-20 Tigershark (jet)

With the Power option (item I), you can specify how powerful an engine you want for your propeller plane or jet. (The sailplane, of course, has no engine.) The propeller plane power is measured in horsepower (HP), and the jet thrust is measured in pounds (lb).

1–5: Rotate

The program displays in three dimensions all visible changes directly on the aircraft pictured on the screen. To obtain an optimal model view, you can rotate the aircraft about its three axes by pressing the 1, 2, or 3 key on the main keypad. Press 1 to yaw the aircraft's heading, press 2 to pitch the aircraft's nose down, and press 3 to bank or roll the aircraft. Once you obtain the desired view, you can stop the picture by pressing the 4 key. To reset the view to the initial position (the side view), press the 5 key.

A–D: Main Wings

*Changing
the wings*

You can change the angle of the wings with respect to the horizontal by pressing the A key and entering the desired number of degrees. Complete the entry by pressing the Esc key. With the B and C options, you can change the span and the aspect ratio in the same way. The aspect ratio specifies the relationship of the length of the wings to the width. Option D provides winglets: wing ends perpendicular to the main wings.

E–G: Stabilizers

You can change the tail configuration of your plane. Specify the size of the vertical section of the tail using option E. Option F lets you position the horizontal section of the tail on the fuselage. To vary the size of the tail area, use option G.

J: Color Design

You can change the color of all visible parts of the aircraft by using submenu J. The aircraft is divided into 10 sections, each of which you can color by selecting the appropriate letter from the menu. Every time you press the key for a section, the program selects and displays a different color. To return to the Aircraft Design menu, press the Esc key.

K: Additional Parameters

Select item K to specify the dry weight, the fuel capacity, and the centers of gravity and lift for your aircraft. You can also specify the aerodynamic characteristics in the frontal area and the landing gear configuration for your design with this option and can name and save the aircraft design. Figure 3.8 shows the Additional Parameters screen.

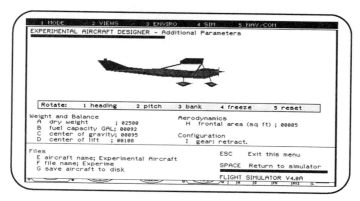

Figure 3.8: Additional Parameters screen

A-D: Weights and Balance

From the Additional Parameters screen, you can specify the dry weight of the aircraft, using option A. You can change the size of the tank and its capacity using option B. You can shift the centers of gravity and lift, thereby changing the stability, using options C and D, respectively.

I: Gear

Use option I to specify whether the landing gear is fixed to the fuselage or retractable.

Frontal Area

Option H lets you modify the aerodynamics of your aircraft by changing the amount of frontal area exposed to the airstream. More area means more air drag and friction; less area means less air drag and friction.

E–G: Files

Select item E to specify a name for your aircraft. To store your new design in the aircraft library, you must save the airplane using item G. The program uses the first eight letters of the name specified under E as the file name. To use a different file name, select option F. To return to the previous submenu, press the Esc key. To go directly to flight mode, press the spacebar.

This step introduces you to a variety of possible views. The program offers not only a standard view from the cockpit, but also a view from a spotter plane. You can get a control-tower perspective or track view, or you can call the map window. Call this menu by pressing the 2 key on the main keypad or selecting option 2, Views, with the mouse. Figure 4.1 shows the Views menu.

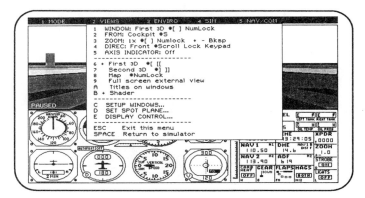

Figure 4.1: Views menu

1: Window

You can display up to three different windows: a map window, which is very useful for navigation and orientation, plus two different 3-D windows. To change the window selected with the Window option, first mark the windows you want displayed by selecting and marking one or more of these options: First 3D, Second 3D, and Map (options 6, 7, and 8). You can activate each window individually and select the particular view you want displayed, the direction of the view, and the amount of magnification. The selected window is distinguished by a white border. Only the windows marked under items 6, 7, and 8 of the View menu can be called with the Window option.

To avoid interrupting your flight every time you select a window, you can call or display windows with the following keys:

- First 3-D window: the [key
- Second 3-D window: the] key
- Map window: the NumLock key

To remove the window, press the appropriate key twice in succession.

You can display several windows on the same screen, as shown in Figure 4.2. If windows overlap during display, you can specify which window is to be placed in the foreground. Choose the desired window and press the ' key.

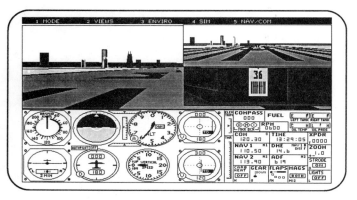

Figure 4.2: Several windows displayed at the same time

2: From

Selecting the point of observation

The From Menu lets you specify a different point of observation for each 3-D window. The following four view modes are available:

Cockpit: Cockpit mode provides the normal view from the aircraft through the cockpit windshield.

Tower: You can follow the takeoff and landing, or simply view the plane, from the perspective of the controller in the tower.

Track: The Track option has two functions, depending on whether you are in single-player or multiplayer mode. In single-player mode, if lets you observe your aircraft from the ground as a tracker. You will be a maximum of 5 miles from the air-craft. In multiplayer mode, this option lets you track the other player's plane.

Spot: You can follow your flight from the view of the pilot of a spotter plane traveling alongside your plane (or behind, or in front of your plane). You set the position of the spotter plane with the Set Spot Plane option discussed later in this step.

3: Zoom

The Zoom option lets you zoom, or change the magnification of, the view in all view modes. Only the active window is affected by the Zoom command. To avoid interrupting your flying session, you can also access the zoom feature by clicking the zoom indicator on the control panel with the mouse or by pressing the + or − key on the main keypad. Pressing the Backspace key restores the magnification to the default setting of 1.0 × Zoom.

4: Direc

The Direc option lets you specify the direction of the view from the cockpit. You can select one of nine possible directions: Front, Right Front, Right, Right Rear, Rear, Left Rear, Left, Left Front, and Down. Panning through the first eight view directions gives you a 360-degree field of view around your plane.

You can choose directions from the keyboard by pressing the Scroll Lock key followed by the view direction (1 to 9) on the numeric keypad. You can also pan the view from your cockpit up in the first eight directions by pressing the Shift and Backspace keys together, and you can pan the view down by pressing the Shift and Enter keys together.

5: Axis Indicator

The axis indicator shows the current axis of the aircraft in the cockpit view mode of a 3-D window. You can display the indicator as a large V-shaped bar, a small V-shaped bar, or four dots in the shape of a diamond, or you can switch the indicator off.

Although the indicator shows where the aircraft center is pointing, this is not necessarily the direction the aircraft is flying.

6: First 3-D W

Turn on the first 3-D window by selecting its option. When the window is on, a + marker appears next to this menu option. You can also switch on the first 3-D window without interrupting the flight by pressing the [key. Press [twice in succession to switch this window off.

7: Second 3-D W

Turn on the second 3-D window by selecting its option or by pressing the] key. When the window is on, a + marker appears next to this menu option. Press the] key twice in succession to turn off this window.

8: Map Window

Select the Map Window option to display the map window. A + marker will appear next to this menu option. You can also toggle the map window on and off by pressing the NumLock key (press the NumLock key twice in succession to turn off the map window).

9: Full-Screen External View

The Full-Screen External View option lets you see a full screen view when the view mode is Tower, Track, or Spot. The airplane instrumentation and controls will disappear to be replaced by a full-screen image of the particular view you have selected.

This command works only for the main or first 3-D window.

A: Titles on Windows

The Titles on Windows option puts the view mode title on the selected window. Titles are especially helpful when you are displaying more than one window.

Displaying titles on windows

B: Shader

The Shader option lets you show aircraft and scenery as lines. When you select this option, the program achieves greater animation speed because it does not need to perform as much computation. A disadvantage of this option, however, is a loss of perception of depth and space.

C: Setup Windows

The Setup Windows option lets you switch on any window and position it on the screen. This option also lets you resize the two 3-D windows and the map window.

As Figure 4.3 shows, you toggle the windows on or off with the 1 to 5 keys. Move into Size mode with the 6, 7, and 8 keys. Enter Move mode with the A to E keys. Change the window size using the numeric keypad and change the window position with the F, T, H, and B keys.

D: Set Spotplane

The Set Spotplane option lets you control the distance and viewing position of the spotter plane that accompanies your airplane. To set the location of the spotter plane in relation to your plane,

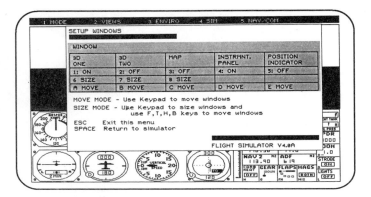

Figure 4.3: The Setup Windows screen

either drag the view box (the small box near the aircraft diagram in the Set Spotplane menu) with the mouse to the desired position or use the numeric keypad direction keys to accomplish this same end.

Use items 1 and 2 on the Set Spotplane menu to set the distance and altitude with respect to the plane. Use item 3 to specify whether the spotter plane is to follow during a loop or a roll. If your plane and the spotter plane are to change sides because of a roll or loop, use menu item 4 to specify whether the spotter plane is to make this transition slowly or quickly.

E: Display Control

Use item 1 of the Display Control submenu to vary how often the program updates and redraws the active windows on the screen. Select the Flicker/Speed Tradeoff menu option. Flicker rate determines how often multiple windows are repainted, and speed determines how often scenery is repainted. Note that with a high clock speed, screen flicker increases. Use item 2 to match the image complexity, or detail, to the corresponding scenery. If, when looking around from the cockpit, you want to make the wings and tail of the airplane invisible, select item 3. Use item 4 to switch the runway approach lighting systems on or off.

Menu 3: Enviro

The Enviro—or Environment—pull-down menu lets you add or change outside environmental effects such as the weather, time of day, season, and air and ground traffic. Select this menu by pressing the 3 key on the main keypad or by selecting option 3 from the main menu with the mouse. Figure 5.1 shows the Enviro menu.

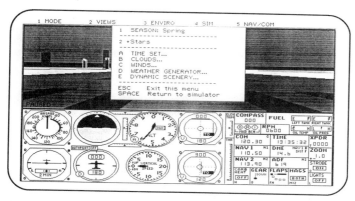

Figure 5.1: Enviro menu

1: Season

When you change the season, you should expect some new difficulties: an icy runway in winter or reduced lift in summer, for example. Under visual flight rules, you must prepare your flight plan to guarantee that you finish the flight by sundown.

Table 5.1 shows the time of transition between the various parts of the day for each season. Note that spring and autumn have the same times.

Season	Dawn	Day	Dusk	Night
Winter	7:00 A.M.	7:30 A.M.	5:00 P.M.	5:30 P.M.
Spring/Autumn	6:00 A.M.	6:30 A.M.	7:00 P.M.	7:30 P.M.
Summer	5:00 A.M.	5:30 A.M.	9:00 P.M.	9:30 P.M.

Table 5.1: Transition Times by Season

2: Stars

Flying at night

The Stars option turns the stars and moon on and off for night displays. The option shows stars of three magnitude levels and places the constellations accurately.

A: Time Set

Setting the time of day

An internal 24-hour clock, which you can set independent of your system time, determines the time of day or night that you are flying. Flight Simulator automatically adjusts the visual flying conditions to correspond to the time of day that appears on this clock. The exact time of transition between dawn, day, dusk, and night varies with the season. Use the Time Set menu (Figure 5.2) to change the displayed time of day.

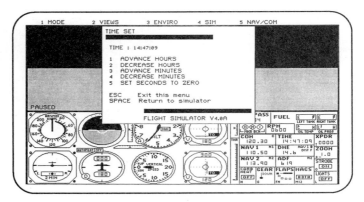

Figure 5.2: Time Set menu

You can also adjust the time with the mouse by pointing to the time control on the instrument panel. Click the left mouse button on the left side of the hours or minutes to decrease the time, and click on the right side to increase the time. Clicking on the right or left of the seconds digits merely resets the seconds to zero.

B: Clouds

You can make your flights more difficult by selecting conditions with reduced visibility or a thunderstorm using the Clouds option. From the Clouds submenu, you can specify two levels of clouds and set the top and base (bottom) limits for each level. The cloud layer altitudes for the top and base are measured in mean feet above sea level. To turn off a cloud layer, you must set the top and base altitudes to zero. The Cover options (options 3 and 7) let you specify the density of cloud cover; the available choices are Clear, Scattered, Broken, and Overcast. You can choose the Deviation options (options 4 and 8) to add a random number to the cloud height, thereby making the appearance of clouds less uniform.

If you turn on options in the Weather Generator menu (option D), the program ignores the clouds set in the Clouds menu.

Flying through a thunderstorm generates some more excitement. You again set a limit for the altitude range, and you specify the strength of the thunderclouds using item B. Specify the direction (in the range 0 to 359 degrees) and the speed (in knots) of the thunderclouds using options C and D. Figure 5.3 shows the Clouds menu.

C: Winds

Flight Simulator offers a comprehensive set of possible wind conditions. You can set different wind configurations for three different altitude levels and on the ground. In each case, specify the wind direction and speed (up to a maximum of 100 knots). Also specify the top and base limits of the wind levels. Specify the strength of turbulence in the individual altitude levels using values from 0 (smooth air) to 10 (severe turbulence).

*Setting
the wind
values*

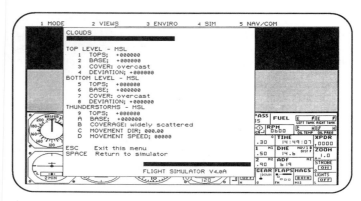

Figure 5.3: Clouds menu

D: Weather Generator

The Weather Generator option is a new feature of Flight Simulator 4.0. You can specify in this menu item unforeseeable changes in the weather, determined by a random weather generator internal to the program. A sudden crosswind during takeoff or landing or an area of poor weather will force pilots to hone their flying skills. The Weather Generator menu offers four options. Option 1, Cloud Buildup, makes clouds build up and dissipate as you fly. Option 2, Front Drift, creates weather fronts that drift through your flight area. Option 3, Wind Changes, randomizes the direction and strength of winds at different altitudes. Option 4, Turbulence Layers, creates air turbulence at different elevations.

Selecting options from the Weather Generator menu disables Cloud menu settings.

E: Dynamic Scenery

The Dynamic Scenery option, new to Flight Simulator 4.0, lets you add air traffic, airport aircraft ground traffic, airport service ground traffic, and miscellaneous other outside airport traffic to make the screen come alive with activity. Airplanes and fuel trucks moving on the apron, aircraft taking off and landing, hot-air balloons on the horizon, and sailboats skipping across the sea are just some of the Dynamic Scenery elements you can see.

Dynamic Scenery is available only for the San Francisco, Chicago O'Hare, and Chicago Meigs areas.

Select the types of objects you want included in your flight session with options 2 through 5. Option 1, Scenery Frequency, lets you have the objects appear sparsely or with medium or complex frequency. Figure 5.4 shows the Dynamic Scenery menu.

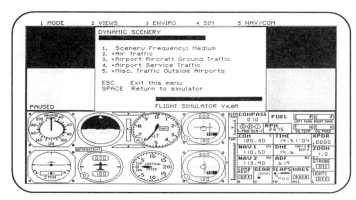

Figure 5.4: Dynamic Scenery menu

Step 6

Menu 4: Sim

15

The Sim—or Simulator—menu lets you alter some of the characteristics of the Flight Simulator program. Features you can control
include program realism; the reliability of instruments and controls; sound; the smoke system; and keyboard, mouse, and joystick sensitivity. To call this menu, select option 4 from the main
menu. Figure 6.1 shows the Sim menu.

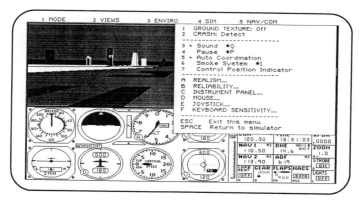

Figure 6.1: Sim menu

1: Ground Texture

The Ground Texture option lets you choose several kinds of randomly placed patterns on the ground to give depth to the scenery.
The choices are Dots, Small Rectangles, Big Rectangles, and Off.

2: Crash

You can choose one of three crash modes that will take effect if
your plane crashes. If you choose the Off option, the plane merely
bounces when it crashes, and you continue flying as if nothing had
happened. The Detect option lets the plane crash (your windshield
will crack) and causes the screen to display a crash message; then

it resets your current flying mode. The Detect and Analysis option also lets your plane crash, but in addition it displays a graph (Figure 6.2) that shows the flight trajectory, vertical velocity, airspeed, and other pertinent information for the last few seconds before the crash; then it resets your current flying mode. Press the Esc key to erase the crash analysis graph and reset the flying mode.

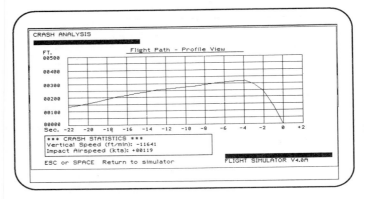

Figure 6.2: Crash analysis graph

3: Sound

Toggle the sound off and on with the Sound option. A plus sign next to the Sound menu listing indicates that the sound is on. You can also toggle the sound on from the keyboard by pressing the Q key.

4: Pause

Halting flight simulator

To interrupt the flight simulation, press the P key or select the Pause option. To resume from where you paused, press P or select Pause again.

5: Auto Coordination

If you select the Auto Coordination option, the program links the rudder and ailerons to one another, letting you coordinate flight movements more easily. When you fly in uncoordinated flight mode, you must control the rudder and ailerons separately. Although this makes flight more difficult, it allows you to perform tricky flight maneuvers not possible when Auto Coordination is selected.

6: Smoke System

To create contrails, or puffs of smoke, at the tail of the aircraft, press the I key or select the Smoke Systems option. These smoke streams are visible from all views and help you track the plane's movement.

7: Control Position Indicator

Choose option 7 to display a separate control position indicator window that shows the position of your plane's elevators, ailerons, rudders, and throttle. You can move this window to any point on the screen by clicking the mouse pointer on the top of the window and, while holding down the left mouse button, dragging the window. You can also move the window by selecting option C, Setup Windows, on the Views menu; selecting option E, Move, on the Setup Windows submenu; and moving the window with the direction keys on the numeric keypad.

A: Realism

To create a realistic flight for the pilot, you can include several realistic effects using the Realism submenu (items A to G). You can also increase the degree of difficulty from easy (1) to realistic (9) with the Flight Control Slide pointer. The pointer below this line shows the current setting. To set the level from the keyboard, press the number you want on the main keypad. Using a mouse, drag the pointer to the setting you want. Figure 6.3 shows the Realism menu.

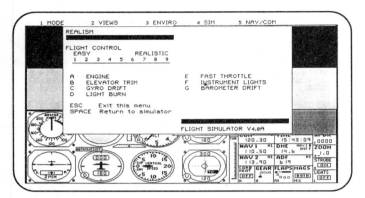

Figure 6.3: Realism menu

A: Engine

If you select the Engine option, you must start or restart the engine using the magneto ignition system. To use the magneto ignition system, press the M and 5 keys.

Note that if you have not yet manually switched your engine off, your engine will continue to run. Only when you next try to restart your engine is the Engine option implemented.

B: Elevator Trim

Finely adjusting the elevator

The elevator trim is a small control surface on the elevators that relieves the pilot of the fatiguing job of continually applying pressure on the yoke to maintain the desired flight path. Usually, the program trims the elevators automatically. If you select the Elevator Trim option, you must set the elevator trim manually because the elevators tend to drift according to aerodynamic conditions.

C: Gyro Drift

Selecting the Gyro Drift option causes the heading indicator to give a false reading. To correct this drift, match the value of the heading indicator to the display of the magnetic compass by pressing the D key.

D: Light Burn

If you select the Light Burn option, your lights may burn out if you leave them on during the day. (Lights also may burn out randomly at any time.)

E: Fast Throttle

If you select the Fast Throttle option, the engine quits if you suddenly apply full throttle.

F: Instrument Lights

If you select the Instrument Lights option, you must switch on the instrument lights at dusk with the L key.

G: Barometer Drift

If you select the Barometer Drift option, you must compensate for false barometer readings from time to time. Press the A key for this purpose.

B: Reliability

Here you specify the degree of reliability of the airplane by entering a number between 1 and 9. You achieve the greatest reliability by entering 9. Press a number key on the main keypad or use the mouse to slide the pointer on the reliability scale.

C: Instrument Panel

To simulate an emergency, you can switch off individual instruments, or all instruments. Figure 6.4 shows the Instrument Panel menu.

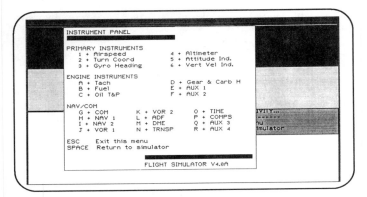

Figure 6.4: Instrument Panel menu

D: Mouse

Adjusting mouse control

The Mouse option lets you set the sensitivity of the control movements when you intend to fly the airplane using a mouse. Press the 1 key to set the sensitivity of yoke motions on a scale from 1 to 8. Then press the Esc key to confirm the set value. Adjust the settings for pointer sensitivity and the yoke null zone in the same way. (The yoke null zone is a center area in the aileron control where the mouse has no effect on the ailerons and the ailerons are automatically centered.) You can also use the mouse to slide the pointer to adjust the mouse sensitivity level. Figure 6.5 shows the Mouse Calibration screen.

E: Joystick

Using the same procedures as for the mouse, you can set the yoke sensitivity, brakes and rudder, throttle, and null zone width for joysticks.

F: Keyboard Sensitivity

The Keyboard Sensitivity option lets you change the sensitivity of the ailerons, elevator, and rudder for keyboard control.

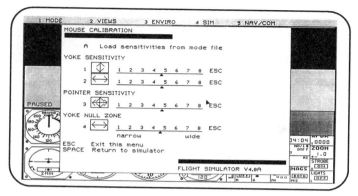

Figure 6.5: Mouse Calibration screen

The Nav/Com—or Navigation and Communication—menu lets you determine or change the present flight position. From this menu, you load other scenery or skip over large distances in a hurry using slewing. This menu also lets you fly with the autopilot and use the electronic flight instrument systems and command flight path display (EFIS/CFPD), the navigation system of the future. Select the Nav/Com menu with the 5 key. Figure 7.1 shows the Nav/Com menu.

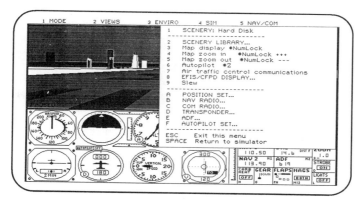

Figure 7.1: Nav/Com menu

1: Scenery: Hard Disk/Floppy Disk in A:

Specify whether the scenery to be loaded is in a subdirectory on the hard disk or on a floppy disk in drive A. You can toggle between the two choices.

2: Scenery Library

Use the Scenery Library option to select the scenery for your flights. If you have a floppy disk of scenery files that you have not yet copied to your hard disk, choose option 1, Scenery in Disk A. Otherwise, pick the scenery file you want from the remaining options. Flight Simulator 4.0 comes with a default scenery disk that includes Chicago, New York and Boston, Seattle, Los Angeles, San Francisco, and the North American continent.

3: Map Display Option

*Opening
a map
window*

To open an additional window containing a map display, select the Map Display option or press the NumLock key. The cross in the center of the map shows your position. To remove the map window, press the NumLock key twice or again select Map Display.

4: Map Zoom In

Use the Map Zoom In option or press the + key on the main keyboard to reduce the scale of the active map window. Using a zoomed in map allows you to display more scenery detail, although you can't see as much area.

5: Map Zoom Out

Select Map Zoom Out to increase the scale of the active map window, or press the – key on the main keyboard.

6: Autopilot

You can toggle the autopilot on or off by selecting Autopilot or by pressing the Z key during a flight. Specify the autopilot parameters under item F, Autopilot Set, in the Nav/Com menu.

7: Air Traffic Control Communications

After choosing the Air Traffic Control Communications option and then pressing the Esc key or spacebar to return to the cockpit, press the Return key. Then specify a request to take off or a request to land, using the Air Traffic Control menu. If, for example, you want to request takeoff clearance from the tower, press Return to activate the Air Traffic Control menu. Then press the 1 key and complete the entry by pressing the Ins key. After a short time, the controller responds and asks you to set the transponder to the required squawk frequency to receive takeoff clearance. When landing, request clearance to land by again pressing Return. Press the 2 key and complete the radio transmission by pressing the Ins key. Figure 7.2 shows the Air Traffic Control menu.

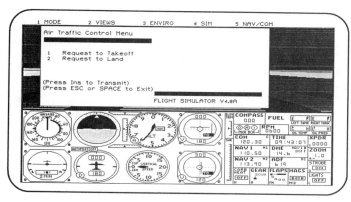

Figure 7.2: Air Traffic Control menu

8: EFIS/CFPD Display

The electronic flight instrument systems and command flight path display (EFIS/CFPD) option turns the EFIS/CFPD navigational aid on and off and lets you select various other parameters. The EFIS/CFPD projects computer-generated symbols on the cockpit windshield to help the pilot land the aircraft and to point out the direction to fly. It projects both the correct flight path and the proper glide slope. Choose the type of path you want displayed with option 2, Type; the available types are Rectangles (you fly through them), Yellow Brick Road (you fly as if driving down a road), and Telephone Poles. To switch EFIS/CFPD on or off, select option 1, Highways, and choose Active or Off. Choose option 3, Density, to specify how densely the displayed path appears.

Choose option 4, Range, to control the distance the path extends in front of you. Figure 7.3 shows the EFIS/CFPD menu.

If you set the Highways option to Active and press the Esc key or spacebar to exit the EFIS/CFPD menu, a new menu appears from which you can select the source for the CFPD to lock on. The CFPD can be locked on to a very high frequency omnidirectional range (VOR) station with the Nav 1 or Nav 2 radio, or it can be locked on to an instrument landing system (ILS) station. Select option 2, Lock to Nav-Aid and Altitude Tracking, to navigate to distant airports or plot a path at a given altitude to some point. Select option 3, Lock to ILS for Landing Approach, to have the CFPD display a path directly to the runway (your Nav 1 or Nav 2 radio must be tuned to the proper ILS frequency, however; see the appendix for a list of ILS runway radio frequencies). To fly a demonstration CFPD landing approach to San Francisco International Airport, select option 1, Fly a Sample CFPD Approach.

9: Slew

The Slew option lets you change your position either rapidly or very delicately and slowly with direct visual control. After you activate slew mode, use the keys listed in Step 2. For more information about slewing, see Step 17.

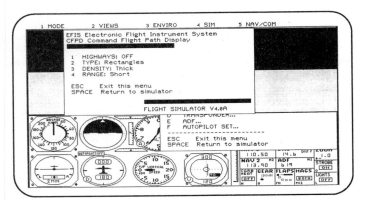

Figure 7.3: EFIS/CFPD menu

A: Position Set

Because flying between distant cities can take hours in real time, Flight Simulator 4.0 offers you a quick way of moving your plane from point to point. Use the Position Set option to directly change your position. Specify your position exactly. Enter the precise north and east coordinates, altitude, and heading, and you can reach any point in the world of Flight Simulator. To help you, the appendix of this book lists the positions of many airports. You also can accurately position the control tower using items 5 to 8, thus changing the view of your aircraft it provides.

B: Nav Radio

Use the Nav Radio option to set navigation radios Nav 1 and Nav 2 and omnibearing heading indicators OBI 1 and OBI 2. Simply select the menu item associated with incrementing or decrementing the control or number you want to set. You can also adjust any number on the instrument panel directly by clicking the mouse on the right (to increase the number) or left (to decrease the number). Option G offers you a choice between the VOR 2 and the automatic direction finder (ADF) display on the instrument panel. Figure 7.4 shows the Nav1/Nav2 submenu; the # sign is followed by the keys you push to accomplish the menu objective.

Setting the Navigational radio

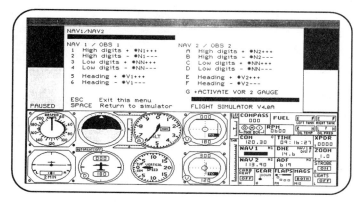

Figure 7.4: Nav1/Nav2 menu

C: Com Radio

To obtain weather or runway information from the automatic terminal information service (ATIS) or to send a message to a flying friend (in multiplayer mode), you set the frequency for the communication radio using the Com Radio option. Figure 7.5 shows the Com Radio menu.

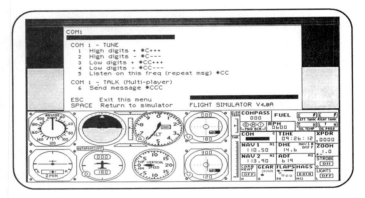

Figure 7.5: Com Radio menu

D: Transponder

Use the transponder, an airborne radio beacon and identifier that responds to radio interrogation signals from air traffic controllers, to rapidly identify your aircraft and increase flight safety. In Flight Simulator, when you are asked by the ground controller to activate your transponder, you will also be given a four-digit "squawk code" that you must set manually on the transponder to identify yourself. You can set the transponder through the Transponder menu, from the keyboard (by pressing T, T T, T T T, and T T T T along with the + or – key to activate the first, second, third, and fourth digits), or with the mouse (repeatedly click the transponder indicator digit you want to change until you reach the correct number).

E: ADF

The task of the automatic direction finder (ADF) is to locate the direction of a selected NDB station (Nondirectional Radio Beacon) and to show it on a display device. Start the ADF display by selecting option 4, activate ADF Gauge, in the ADF menu. This display replaces the second lower OBI for the Nav 2 radio in the instrument panel. Specify the frequency code using options 1 to 3.

Using the automatic direction finder

F: Autopilot Set

The autopilot is an aid used to fly a preset course or an altitude automatically. Use options 3 and 4 to set the desired heading and altitude. Alternatively, select option 2, Nav 1 Lock. The autopilot then navigates to the selected VOR station tuned on your Nav 1 radio. To counteract possible air turbulence, use option 1, the wing leveler. To toggle the autopilot on and off, select option 5 or press the Z key during a flight.

The cockpit of an airplane contains many instruments, displays, and navigational equipment. The following chapter describes the standard instrument cluster in detail. It briefly mentions the flight instruments and indicators and the radio and navigational equipment because these are discussed in later steps.

Learning your way around the cockpit

Standard Instrument Cluster

The six primary flight instruments, the standard instrument cluster, can be divided into two categories: pressure instruments and gyroscopic instruments. The gyroscopic instruments include the turn coordinator, the directional gyro, and the artificial horizon. The pressure instruments include the airspeed indicator, the vertical speed indicator, and the altimeter. Figure 8.1 shows the cockpit instrument panel.

The Gyroscopic Instruments

The gyroscope instruments provide information about the aircraft's direction and attitude.

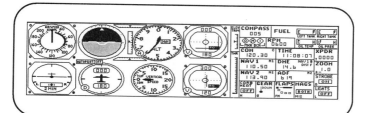

Figure 8.1: The instrument panel

Turn Coordinator (Turn and Bank Indicator)

Specifying the turning rate

The turn coordinator, shown in Figure 8.2, has two functions. It measures turn rate, and it measures the amount of slip or skid the aircraft has in making a turn.

For example, suppose you want to make a standard left turn with a turn rate of 3 degrees per second (thus completing a 360-degree turn in 2 minutes). The wing tip of the airplane symbol must align with the "L" mark on the indicator, and after a specified or predetermined amount of time, you will have completed a standard turn for a given angle.

Using the ball level

The ball level is below the airplane symbol on the indicator. If the ball of the display does not move from the center position while you are turning, you are making the turn with the correct bank and turn rate; the forces are in balance. However, if the ball moves out of the center position, it suggests a sloppy turn (slip and skid). (In auto-coordination mode, you generally don't need to worry about coordination with the ball level.)

Artificial Horizon

The artificial horizon, shown in Figure 8.3, tells the pilot the airplane's attitude at all times. It shows the actual pitch and roll of the aircraft in relation to the ground. The instrument thus provides the view of the natural horizon that the pilot would have during a visual flight.

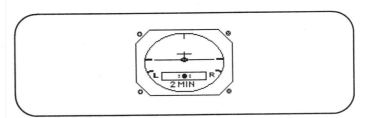

Figure 8.2: The turn coordinator

The principal component of the artificial horizon is a gimbal-mounted gyroscope. This gyroscope retains its position in space regardless of changes in the course and position of the aircraft. The horizontal line on the gyroscope thus remains parallel to the natural horizon with the aircraft in any position. Dots marked 10°, 20°, 30°, 60°, and 90° on the front of the instrument show the aircraft's angle of bank. The scale in the center of the display symbolizes the aircraft by its center point.

Structure of the artificial horizon

Directional Gyro

The directional gyro, or heading indicator, shown in Figure 8.4, shows the direction of the airplane. There is one essential difference between this instrument and the magnetic compass: the directional gyro provides a precise, instantaneous display of the course even when the aircraft experiences pronounced acceleration forces or vibrations (during climbing, looping, and so on). A disadvantage of the directional gyro is the slow drift of the gyro

Displaying the course

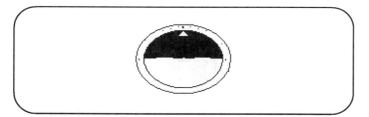

Figure 8.3: The artificial horizon

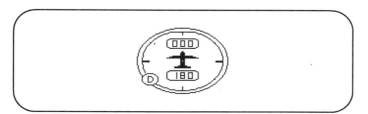

Figure 8.4: The directional gyro

plane. Compare the display of the directional gyro to that of the magnetic compass during horizontal straight flight without acceleration. Compensate for any deviation of the directional gyro by pressing the D key.

The Pressure Instruments

The pressure instruments obtain their information from a dynamic air-pressure system and a static air-pressure system.

Airspeed Indicator

The airspeed indicator, shown in Figure 8.5, measures, in knots, the aircraft's speed through the air—not the ground speed. The airspeed readings are obtained from a dynamic air pressure measurement, and are thus susceptible to fluctuations in air pressure, temperature, and weather.

Altimeter

Scale division

When calibrated, the altimeter shows the altitude over mean sea level (MSL). Air pressure constantly decreases as altitude increases. By measuring this pressure, the instrument determines and displays the altitude, measured in feet. Calibrate the altimeter to the local atmospheric pressure with the A key. The instrument display is comparable to that of a clock. The small ticks on the dial represent steps of 20 feet for the large hand and 200 feet for the small hand. The large hand indicates the altitude in steps of 100 feet. The small pointer displays steps of 1000 feet. The circle

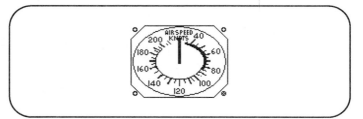

Figure 8.5: The airspeed indicator

on the edge of the scale has steps of 10,000 feet. Figure 8.6 shows the altimeter.

Vertical Speed Indicator

The vertical velocity indicator, shown in Figure 8.7, specifies the rate at which the aircraft is climbing or descending. The display is calibrated in units of hundreds of feet per minute (FPM). The dial shows a reading of 0 to 20 up or down, signifying a climb or descent of 0 to 2000 feet per minute. However, when you are flying the Gates Learjet, the vertical speed indicator is recalibrated to read speeds up to 8000 feet per minute (0 to 8 on the recalibrated dial) if you are using display driver options H or M, EGA or VGA 16-Color 640×350 from the Setup menu.

It is not practical for pilots to regularly respond to this display, because the vertical velocity indicator reacts only after a slight delay. Responding thus would cause unsteady, uncoordinated flight.

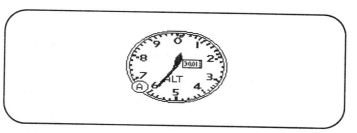

Figure 8.6: The altimeter

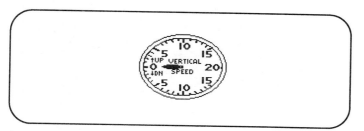

Figure 8.7: The vertical speed indicator

Other Flight Instruments and Indicators

The cockpit also contains other instruments and indicators that supply information about the status of the aircraft.

Navigational Instruments

Several instruments aid in navigation.

Magnetic Compass

The magnetic compass display shows your current heading.

Outer, Middle, and Inner Marker Lights

The marker beacon gives a visual signal when you fly over the outer (O), middle (M), or inner markers (I) of the instrument landing system (ILS) for a particular runway.

OBI 1 with Glidescope

The omnibearing indicator 1 (OBI 1) navigational instrument is used with the Nav 1 radio, which tunes in VOR radio beacons or ILS stations. It also contains a glidescope indicator with moving cross-hairs that is indispensable for landing the aircraft under instrument flying conditions using ILS radio guidance stations tuned on the Nav 1 radio. Figure 8.8 shows OBI 1.

OBI 2/ADF

The omnibearing indicator 2 automatic direction finder (OBI 2/ADF) is identical to OBI 1 except it is used with the Nav 2 radio and it does not come with a glidescope indicator. The OBI 2 can be switched off and replaced by a second navigational instrument: the ADF. Figure 8.8 also shows OBI 2.

Other Indicators

Figure 8.9 shows the indicator panel.

Fuel, Oil Temp, and Oil Pressure Indicators

The fuel gauges for the left and right tanks display the amount of fuel available for your flight; the needle moves from full to empty.

Figure 8.8: OBI 1 and OBI 2

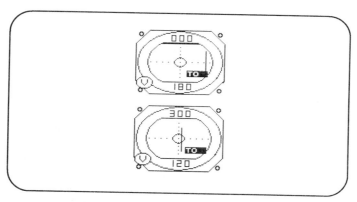

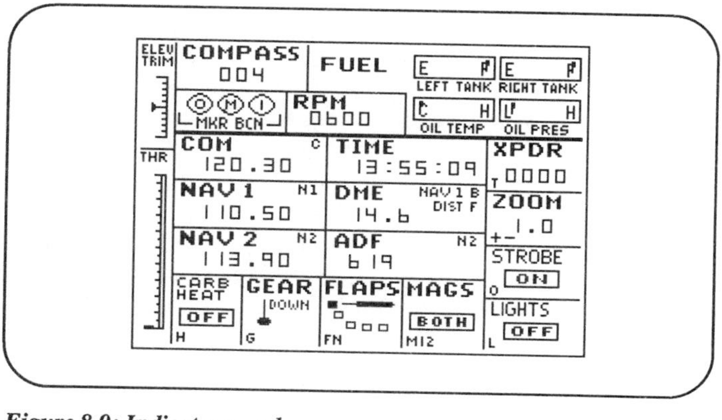

Figure 8.9: Indicator panel

The oil temperature indicator displays the oil temperature; the needle moves from cold to hot. The oil pressure display indicates whether the oil pressure is too low or too high.

RPM Tachometer

The tachometer shows the engine speed per minute in a digital display. For the Cessna, the engine speed is measured in RPM, or rotations per minute, and for the Gates Learjet, engine speed is measured in percentage of RPM.

Time

Time is shown on a standard digital clock measuring hours, minutes, and seconds in real time. To reset the clock, select option A, Time Set, on the Enviro pull-down menu, or click the digits on the clock with the mouse.

Zoom

The zoom indicator shows the current magnification, or zoom factor, of the view in the selected 3-D window. This zoom indicator does not work with the map, contrary to the Flight Simulator documentation.

Strobe and Lights Switches

The strobe switch turns on and off the flashing red strobe light beacon mounted on the aircraft tail. The lights switch turns on and off the running lights and instrument lights.

Carb Heat/Spoilers

The carburetor heat switch turns the carburetor heat on and off. Use carburetor heating to prevent icing or to clear ice that has formed in the carburetor, thus preventing ice-caused engine failure in cold weather.

When you are flying the Gates Learjet, the carburetor heat control is replaced by a spoilers control that increases drag and acts like an air brake. You can see the spoiler control only if you are using display driver options H or M, EGA or VGA 16-Color 640×350, on the Setup menu.

Gear

The landing gear display indicates whether the landing gear is up or down.

Flaps

Flaps are moveable wing panels that are hinged so that they can move up or down to increase or decrease lift and drag on the aircraft. The Flaps can be extended in 10-degree increments up to 40 degrees.

Mags/Engs

The magneto indicator specifies whether you have switched on the left, the right, or both magnetos (engine ignition coils).

When you are flying the Gates Learjet, the magneto indicator is replaced by the engines indicator, which allows you to control the two General Electric CJ610-8A turbojets, thus giving you the option of flying with just the right or left engine. As with the spoiler indicator, the engine indicator appears only if you are using display driver options H or M, EGA or VGA 16-Color 640×350, on the Setup menu.

Control Position Indicators

The control position indicators on the instrument panel show the current position of the ailerons, elevators, and rudder (the yoke controls; see Figure 8.10); the elevator trim; and the throttle.

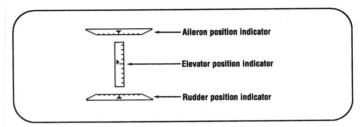

Figure 8.10: Yoke control position indicators

Aileron Position Indicator

The moveable hinged surfaces on the trailing edge of each wing are called ailerons. They control the rotational movement known as banking or roll.

Elevator Position Indicator

The elevators are moveable hinged control surfaces on the horizontal stabilizer (the tail wing). They control the up or down pitch of the aircraft's nose.

Rudder Position Indicator

The rudder is the hinged vertical control surface mounted on the trailing edge of the vertical stabilizer (the tail). It controls the rotational movement known as yaw (right or left pivoting motion).

Elevator Trim Indicator

The elevator trim allows fine adjustment of the elevators. (The elevator trim indicator is located above the throttle indicator; see Figure 8.9.)

Throttle (THR) Position Indicator

The THR indicator shows how much throttle has been applied to the engines.

Radios

Flight Simulator uses two types of radios: navigational radios and communications radios.

Navigational Radios

Use the navigational radios to guide your aircraft.

Nav1/Nav2

The Nav 1 and Nav 2 radio receivers are used for navigation and tune in either VOR or ILS radio stations. The displays for the receivers are OBI 1 and OBI 2. You also use the Nav 1 receiver for the instrument landing system and for the EFIS/CFPD advanced navigational graphics display system.

Nav 1 works with the OBI 1 display, and Nav 2 works with the OBI 2 display.

DME

Together with the Nav receiver, the distance measuring equipment (DME) shows the distance or speed to or from a VOR in nautical miles. Note that in the upper-right corner of the DME box, you can toggle the Nav 1 or Nav 2 radio as your selected VOR station. To toggle between groundspeed and distance, press the F key.

XPNDR

Enter your transponder (xpndr) identification number for air traffic control so that controllers can identify your aircraft on radar.

ADF

The automatic direction finder (ADR) radio receiver for nondirectional beacons is used in conjunction with the ADF display that can be called up to replace the OBI 2 display.

Communications Radios

Use communications radios to talk to the ground.

Com

Using the Com receiver, you can enter the frequency for the Automatic Terminal Information Service (ATIS). Call ATIS up again to the screen as a moving (horizontally scrolling) message with the C key. See the appendix for a list of ATIS frequencies for selected airports.

In this step you will learn about taxiing and how to call up weather information and air traffic control. You will also perform your first takeoff. Before starting this step, make sure Flight Simulator is configured to work with your particular computer, monitor, keyboard, and mouse or joysticks. Start Flight Simulator by typing **FS4** at the DOS prompt. When the program loads, you should have a cockpit view of Chicago Meigs Field runway 36 from your Cessna Skylane RG II airplane (see Figure 9.1). In the background you should hear the steady drone of your engines idling.

If you want to take off right away, you can skip the next three sections on taxiing, weather information, and air traffic control and go directly to the takeoff checklist.

Taxiing

This section gives you some practice in taxiing down the runway and returning to your original start position poised for takeoff. Take a moment to learn how to use your 360-degree field of view out the cockpit windows to better orient yourself on the ground.

Different cockpit views

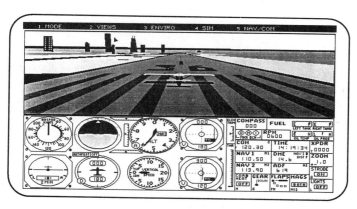

Figure 9.1: Runway 36 at Chicago Meigs Field

At first, your view out the window is the front view; you will see runway 36 stretching in front of you into the horizon. Press the Scroll Lock key and the 7 key on the numeric keypad to see out the right front window. In the same way, pressing first the Scroll Lock key followed by the 4, 1, 2, 3, 6, 9, and 8 number keys, you can look out each of the eight possible views that make up your field of vision. Return to a front view by pressing the Scroll Lock key and then the 8 key.

The map window

Next, call up the map window so you can easily see where you are in relation to the other runways and buildings of the airport. Press the NumLock key to bring up the map and then use the + and − keys on the main keyboard to zoom in and zoom out. This procedure will allow you to get a good view of your position at the airport and of where you need to go. The center cross on the map represents your airplane. You press NumLock twice in succession to remove the map. For now, though, keep the map displayed.

Begin taxiing (see Figure 9.2) down the runway by increasing your throttle to 881 RPM. To do this, press the 9 key on the numeric keypad five times. Steering the airplane is accomplished with the rudder controls (0 and the bottom-right keys on the numeric keypad), which on the ground also steer your plane's nose wheel. Press the 5 key to quickly center the rudder and nose

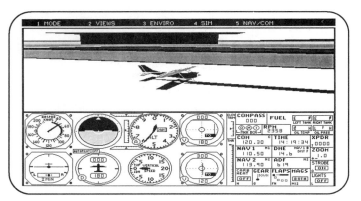

Figure 9.2: Taxiing

wheel. Keep rolling down the runway until you see a turnoff runway on your left. Take this turnoff and proceed straight until you see another left turnoff. Once again make a left turn and taxi straight until you see the turnoff for the main runway where you started. After you take this turnoff, you will return to runway 36. You will be ready to take off once you have reoriented your plane to point in the right direction. To come to a complete stop, cut the throttle by pressing the 3 key on the numeric keypad and apply your brakes by pressing the . key on the main keypad. Don't worry if you are at first unsuccessful at taxiing or are unable to return your plane to its original position; these movements take some practice. If your plane is not ready to take off on runway 36, press the PrtScr key, and the simulator will reset itself.

Getting Weather Information

Using ATIS

To obtain the latest information about the airport weather and your landing strip assignment, you can call up the Automatic Terminal Information Service (ATIS) on Com frequency 121.30 MHz. Press the C key and the + key to set the integer digits. Press the C key twice and the − key to set the decimal digits. To call up ATIS again, press the C key again.

The following information appears on your screen:

Scrolling Message on Screen	Explanation
Meigs Field Information X-Ray	ATIS station identification
13.00 Zulu	1:00 p.m. universal time
Weather	Weather
Visibility 10	Visibility 10 miles
Temperature 14	Temperature 63° Fahrenheit
Wind 00 at 0	Wind from the north and calm

Scrolling Message on Screen	*Explanation*
`Altimeter 29.95`	Air pressure: 29.95 inches of Hg
`Landing and departing runway 36`	Landing and departing on runway 36
`Advise controller that you have x-ray 36`	Contact controller for permission to land or take off.

Getting Air Traffic Control Clearance

Before you take off or land, you must request takeoff clearance from the tower. To do this, select the air traffic control communication option in the Nav/Com menu (menu 5). Exit this menu by pressing Esc. Then press the Return key to display the Air Traffic Control menu. On this menu, select item 1, Request to Takeoff, and transmit the message to the tower by pressing the Ins key. Follow the instructions of the controller for taxi and takeoff clearance and set the transponder to the required squawk code. As soon as you receive clearance from the tower and set your transponder, go through the takeoff checklist.

Performing a Takeoff Check

Before taking off, you must go through the takeoff checklist. By briefly moving the controls, check the elevators, rudders, and ailerons. Examine the instruments and displays one last time. Check these items:

The takeoff checklist

Indicator	*Setting*
Magnetos	Both checked
Throttle	600 RPM
Oil pressure and temperature	Gauge indicators centered
Fuel	Right and left tank full
Carburetor heat	On for takeoff and landings

Indicator	*Setting*
Flaps	10°
Elevator trim	Centered
Rudder, elevators, and ailerons	Centered
Directional gyro	Press D to calibrate if necessary

When the checklist is completed, you are ready for takeoff.

Taking Off

Increase the throttle to 881 RPM by pressing the 9 key on the numeric keypad five times. The aircraft will begin to move slowly down the runway. Align the Cessna on the center line of the runway by pressing the 0 and bottom-right keys on the numeric keypad. (These keys control the right and left movement of your steering wheel on the ground.) In auto-coordination mode (the default mode in this case), the ailerons are linked with the rudders, so you can also steer with the 4 and 6 keys or the mouse. To quickly center the rudders, ailerons, or steering wheel, press the 5 key.

You have already set the flaps to the 10-degree position for greater lift, so you are set to take off. Use full throttle for maximum takeoff speed. Strong crosswinds often make a calm and controlled takeoff difficult. Counteract this drift by carefully applying the rudder and ailerons. Try not to zigzag by moving the rudder and ailerons excessively and do not hesitate to abort the takeoff if you see that you cannot take off safely. To abort, decrease the throttle to 600 RPM by pressing the 3 key on the numeric keypad and apply the brakes by repeatedly pressing the . key on the main keypad.

Getting Airborne

As you accelerate down the runway, keep an eye on your airspeed indicator. At a speed of about 70 knots per hour, the aircraft will lift off from the runway without your raising the nose of the airplane with the elevators. The Microsoft *Instruction Manual* erroneously states that you need to rotate or pull the yoke back slowly to achieve lift off. This is incorrect, as the aircraft will take off unassisted by any yoke movement so long as your elevators are centered.

Notice that the altimeter and the vertical velocity indicator display a constant increase in altitude. After you have overflown the end of the runway, retract the landing gear with the G key to reduce air resistance. Once you have gained a little altitude, you must also retract your flaps to the up or 0-degree position by pressing the appropriate function key for your keyboard or using the mouse.

It is always best to take off into the wind if possible, because the wind speed adds to the takeoff speed and so reduces your takeoff distance. Figure 9.3 shows the screen as the plane takes off.

Steps to a Successful Takeoff

Summary

Here again are the most important steps to a successful takeoff:

1. Align the Cessna on the center line of the runway.

2. Make sure all yoke and elevator trim control position indicators are centered.

3. Extend the flaps 10 degrees.

4. Slowly increase the throttle to maximum.

5. After you accelerate to approximately 70 knots per hour, the plane will lift off by itself, without any interference from the pilot.

6. Retract the flaps and the landing gear once you are safely airborne.

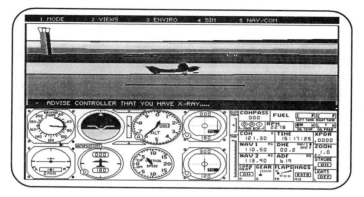

Figure 9.3: Taking off

Step 10

Climbing

Step 10 discusses climbing: the transition between takeoff and cruising altitude. Flight Simulator distinguishes three phases of climbing: entry, climbing, and leveling off. After this step, you will be able to make the transition from a stable climb to steady horizontal flight.

Entry Phase

If you took off as directed in Step 9, you should be climbing steadily without making any adjustments to the controls except that you should have retracted the flaps and landing gear. An optimal rate of climb just after takeoff is about 900 feet per minute (FPM). You should soon see the vertical speed indicator move to 9 on the gauge. The maximum rate of climb for the Cessna at sea level is 1050 FPM (this number is affected by altitude, aircraft speed, and weather). After you reach the desired altitude, reduce the throttle and level the airplane with the elevators.

Climbing Phase

To achieve a constant climb of about 900 FPM, you should use full throttle. You need not adjust your elevators to change your climb rate, because the plane will climb without any intervention on your part. Watch the pointer on the vertical elevator trim display. This pointer should be centered. You can fine tune the elevator trim with the 1 and 7 keys on the numeric keypad to make minute adjustments to your climb rate. The vertical velocity indicator will level off at about 900 FPM. With these selected values, your airspeed is about 70 knots. Because the aircraft is somewhat slow to respond, a slight delay will occur before you reach the desired values.

With a high rate of climb, low speed, and full throttle, the aircraft may turn to the left (yaw). React by actuating the right rudder. If you encounter turbulence, stabilize your plane with the ailerons.

Figure 10.1 shows the screen during the climbing phase.

Accommodating Decreasing Lift

As altitude increases, air density decreases, and so lift also decreases. To accommodate this steady decrease in lift, you must regulate the climb by changing the throttle and by changing the pitch of the aircraft using the elevator. Your maximum rate of climb decreases with increasing altitude.

Changing the Rate of Climb

As soon as you have reached the minimum altitude required by the FAA, you can change to a more pleasant, lower rate of climb. You achieve the desired results by regulating the throttle and the elevator setting.

Remember, however, that you will not have sufficient lift if your speed is too low or your rate of climb is too high. Insufficient lift can cause your plane to stall (see Figure 10.2). The flight simulator reacts to this condition with an audible warning and a stall indicator message on the right side of the cockpit windshield (see Figure 10.3). Do not panic and do not make any sudden changes.

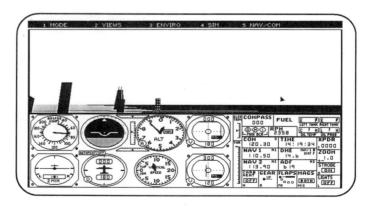

Figure 10.1: The climbing phase

Figure 10.2: External view of a stall

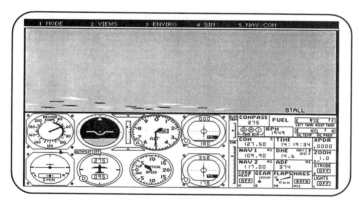

Figure 10.3: The stall warning

The best way to recover from this situation is to lower the nose to regain flying speed and then return to straight and level flight.

Leveling Off Phase

Before attaining cruising altitude, or target altitude, you must gently level the airplane to bring it into stable, horizontal flight. Lower the nose by lowering the elevator. Start this transition from

*Transition
to straight
and level
flight*

a climb to straight and level flight well before you reach cruising altitude. Decrease the throttle slowly while watching your vertical speed indicator move to 0 FPM. Your artificial horizon should be level and centered. Only when an equilibrium exists between the elevator position and the throttle setting will your plane fly in a straight and level path.

Figure 10.4 shows the screen as you level off your aircraft.

Achieving straight and level flight

After the transition from climbing to straight and level flight, the horizon line must be located exactly in the center of the artificial horizon display. Also, the vertical velocity indicator must show a value of zero. You should observe an increase in horizontal speed as you look at the airspeed indicator. This increase results from the conversion of climbing speed into additional horizontal speed.

Remember, now, to trim the elevators again, because the increase in speed creates additional lift forces.

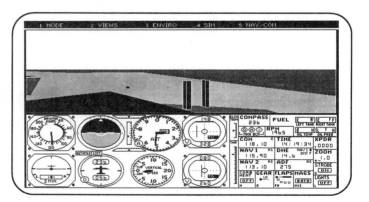

Figure 10.4: Leveling off your aircraft

Steps from Entry to Level Flight

1. Open the throttle to 2358 RPM, making sure the flaps and landing gear are retracted.

2. Maintain a constant airspeed of 70 knots, keeping the rate of climb at 900 FPM.

3. Change from climbing to straight and level flight by lowering the nose while simultaneously reducing the throttle.

4. Check the elevator indicator, artificial horizon, and vertical velocity indicator.

5. Use the elevator trim to fine-tune nose pitch.

Summary

Flying Straight &Level

After you complete a climb, you make the transition to straight and level flight by reducing the throttle and lowering the elevators. Start the transition well before you reach your desired cruising altitude, because some time is needed to stabilize the aircraft.

Flying at Cruising Altitude

The most important condition for maintaining straight and level flight is keeping the altitude within 100 feet of the cruising altitude—the standard value for flying straight and level (S&L).

Because full throttle is not necessary when flying straight and level, decrease the engine speed to 2302 RPM. This way, you achieve the standard cruising speed of 130 knots.

Do not attempt to compensate for a drop in altitude by forcefully moving the elevators. If you lose altitude, increase the throttle. If you gain altitude, decrease the throttle.

Standard Instrument Readings

When you achieve cruising altitude, your instrument panel should display the following values (shown in Figure 11.1):

Instrument	Value
Airspeed indicator	130 knots
Vertical velocity indicator	0 FPM
RPM	2302 RPM
Turn and bank indicator	Horizontal flight, wings centered
Artificial horizon	Horizontal flight, shaded horizon centered on gull wing marker in center of dial and roll pointer centered

Checking the flight values

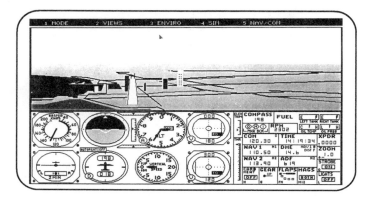

Figure 11.1: Flying straight and level

After attaining these values, you can sit back, relax, and enjoy the beautiful scenery. However, check your instruments periodically to make sure that you are not losing or gaining altitude, and that your heading remains constant.

Cross-Checking the Instruments

The basis for a safe flight using instruments is continual monitoring of the most important instruments. Start the cross-check with the most important instrument: the artificial horizon. Then read the current altitude on the altimeter. After looking at the artificial horizon again, check the speed on the airspeed indicator. Finally, check your course using the compass.

Press the NumLock key to call up the map, press the + and - keys on the main keypad to zoom in and out, and press the Scroll Lock and 1 through 9 key combinations to observe out your various side windows.

Making Turns

15

The turn is one of the basic flight maneuvers that every pilot must master. You make turns by banking the wings. Indeed, for safe instrument flight, you must be able to perform course corrections precisely.

There are three types of turns: shallow, medium, and steep.

- Shallow turns have a bank angle of less than 20 degrees. The plane tends to drift back to level flight unless you apply more aileron.

- Medium turns have a bank angle between 20 and 45 degrees. The plane will continue to turn without any additional application of the ailerons.

- Steep turns have a bank angle of more than 45 degrees. The plane continues to bank ever more steeply unless you counter this tendency by reversing the ailerons.

Making a Standard Turn

The turn indicator, as discussed in Step 8, measures turn rate and coordination. When the wings of the plane symbol in the gauge align with the L (left) or R (right) indicator, the plane will make what is known as a standard turn: in 2 minutes the plane will complete a 360-degree turn and be headed once again in the same direction. Such a turn has a turn rate of 3 degrees per second. But in order to bank or roll the aircraft the proper angle for a standard turn, you must also take into account the airspeed of the plane. The following rule of thumb allows you to accurately calculate your bank angle for a standard turn:

Bank angle in degrees (standard turn) = (Airspeed in knots/10) + 7

Starting the Turn

Once you have computed the integer value for the bank angle, start the standard turn by gently applying the ailerons. Observe your artificial horizon banking indicator, noting that the small arrow at the top of the gauge will be pointing at one of the 0°, 20°, 30°, 60°, or 90° banking marker dots. When you have reached the appropriate bank angle, center the ailerons to prevent the airplane from rolling or banking further.

Assessing the turn

Now you must monitor your altitude. You can maintain cruising altitude only by raising the nose or increasing the throttle. If the bank angle is correct, the wing tip of the turn and bank indicator will point to the appropriate position (L or R). The ball level should be at the center, showing that you are flying a clean standard turn with the required banking speed.

Centering the ailerons

As soon as you have brought the wings of the turn and bank indicator to the L or R mark, neutralize the ailerons by centering them. In a shallow turn, the aircraft will tend to stabilize itself to level flight, so if necessary, add more aileron to sustain the bank angle.

Figure 12.1 shows the screen as you start a standard turn.

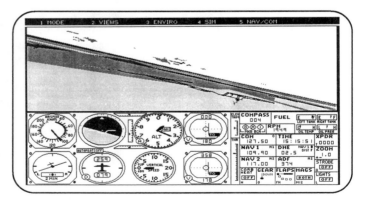

Figure 12.1: Starting a standard turn

You now are flying a standard turn with a banking speed of 3 degrees per second. At the beginning of the turn, check the clock on the instrument panel. A standard turn will last precisely 2 minutes. This means that in 1 minute you will have flown a semicircle of 180 degrees.

If the banking speed increases or decreases due to external influences (for example, wind), correct the bank angle with the help of the artificial horizon.

Ending a Standard Turn

To reach the desired heading, you must roll out of the turn at the right time. Calculate this roll-out point using the following equation:

Integer degree value for beginning the rollout = Bank angle/2

For example, suppose you are flying a standard turn with a bank angle of 20 degrees at a speed of about 130 knots. If you divide the bank angle by 2 (20/2 = 10 degrees), you must start the rollout 10 degrees before reaching the desired course, using the artificial horizon as an aid.

Figure 12.2 shows the screen as you complete a standard turn.

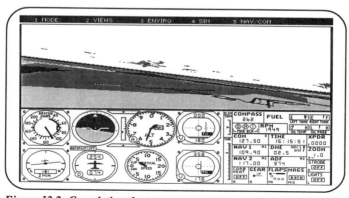

Figure 12.2: Completing the turn

After you finish the turn, lower the nose slightly, using the elevator to return to straight and level flight. Make sure that your artificial horizon is level, and that the aircraft is neither gaining nor losing altitude.

Step 13

Descending & Landing

This step explains how to descend and safely land the Cessna Sky-lane RG II airplane. These flight maneuvers are complex, so do not expect to completely master this step without devoting more than the suggested time. You will need to practice descending and landing many times, as the procedures are involved and tricky. Fortunately, Flight Simulator 4.0 comes with an excellent practice flight mode, called Oakland 27R—Landing Approach.

Oakland 27R—Landing Approach

After loading Flight Simulator, select the Mode pull-down menu and then press the B key to begin switching to the other flight mode options. Keep pressing the B key until you get to the Oakland 27R—Landing Approach mode. If you have recently switched mode libraries, you must call up the library that contains Oakland 27R by selecting option F, Mode Library. Then call up the other available flight modes by selecting option 7, See More Modes. Once Oakland 27R—Landing Approach is selected, you are ready to start the simulator by pressing the spacebar.

Planning Your Landing

Before leaving cruising altitude, you must first thoroughly plan your landing, because a perfect landing depends on careful planning. Interrupt the Flight Simulator program with the P key. You will now have enough time to perform a cross-check and to calculate the rate of descent.

Pausing Flight Simulator to plan your landing

Checking Weather and Runway Condition Information

Summon weather information and runway conditions by tuning your COM radio to the Oakland ATIS (Automatic Terminal Information Service), on a frequency of 126.0 Mhz. The message that soon scrolls across your windshield gives you information helpful in planning your approach and landing.

Cross-Checking

Even though the simulator is still paused, take a few moments to read your instruments using the cross-check method. Start with the altimeter. You are 1200 feet above mean sea level (MSL). Oakland Airport is 13 feet above sea level, so you are actually 1187 feet above ground level (AGL). Be careful to distinguish between MSL and AGL because at higher-elevation airports, your altimeter MSL readings may tempt you to think that you have plenty of altitude above the ground, when in fact you may be hurtling toward the ground. Next, check your airspeed indicator reading of 80 knots and then your engine speed of 1949 RPM. The artificial horizon and the turn and bank indicator confirm that you are flying straight and level. The vertical speed indicator should initially show that your rate of climb or descent is about zero. Your directional gyro shows that you are on the correct course heading of 275 degrees. Your flaps are set at 10 degrees, and your landing gear is extended. Last, glance at your DME indicator, which shows that you are 3.7 miles from the runway. Figure 13.1 shows the starting position for the landing.

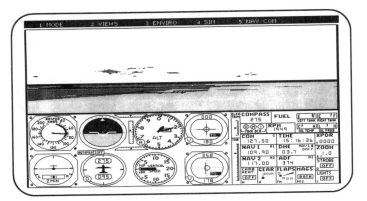

Figure 13.1: Starting position for landing

Calculating the Rate of Descent

When you start in the Oakland 27R—Landing Approach mode, you are 3.7 miles away from the runway and flying at about

80 knots (1.33 nautical miles per minute), which means you will touch down in about 3 minutes. Accordingly, you must decrease your altitude from 1200 feet MSL within 3 minutes, which requires a rate of descent of 400 feet per minute (FPM). In the scenario here, however, we will use a steeper glide angle of 700 to 800 FPM to position the plane a little in front of the runway, for practice purposes.

Starting Your Descent

Resume the simulation by pressing the P key. Immediately reduce the engine speed to 1499 RPM by pressing the 3 key on the numeric keypad until you have reached this value (alternatively, use the mouse to reduce the throttle). Next, lower your elevators by repeatedly pressing the 8 key on the numeric keypad so that the nose of the plane begins to pitch downward and the vertical speed indicator shows a downward movement. Use the elevator gingerly, because only slight movements can cause great changes in nose pitch. When your vertical speed indicator settles at 700 to 800 FPM, you must again readjust your elevators upward with the 2 key to stabilize your descent and prevent it from becoming steeper.

Using Elevator Trimming to Correct Vertical Speed

As the air pressure increases with decreasing altitude or temperature changes, you must constantly observe the rate of descent using the vertical speed indicator and the altimeter. Correct or compensate by using the elevator trim, pressing the 7 and 1 keys on the numeric keypad.

Using Ailerons to Correct Heading

Regularly check your heading on the compass. Runway 27R is at a course heading of 275 degrees. If you deviate from the desired course, correct the heading by moving the ailerons slightly with the 4 and 6 keys on the numeric keypad.

Course: 275°

Turning on Carburetor Heat and Lights

Turn on the carburetor heat with the H key (or mouse) to prevent
ice-caused engine failure on a landing approach. Your engine
speed will decrease to 1419 RPM, which is fine. You should also
turn on your lights with the L key (or the mouse).

Performing a Final Check

Quickly perform a final check of the following instruments and
values:

Carburetor heat	On
Flaps	10°
Landing gear	Down
Lights	On
Course	275°
Airspeed	95 to 100 knots
Vertical speed	700 to 800 FPM
Engine speed	1419 RPM (with carburetor heat on)

Figure 13.2 shows the instrument panel during descent.

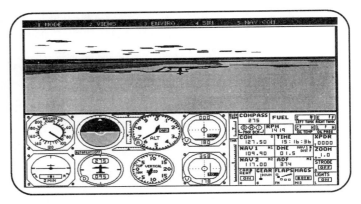

Figure 13.2: Instrument display during descent

Making the Final Landing Approach

At a distance of about ½ mile from the runway (observe the DME indicator for closing distance), your altitude should be 120 to 200 feet MSL. Increase your throttle to approximately 1588 RPM to decrease your vertical speed to between 200 and 500 FPM. Do not use your elevators to adjust your descent rate, because increasing or decreasing your engine thrust will accomplish the same end. Your airspeed should be 80 to 90 knots at this point. Try to maintain this speed and rate of descent for the entire landing approach.

Under no circumstances should you let the speed drop below 54 knots, because at speeds less than this, the plane will stall and lose maneuverability. Remember that your vertical speed during this phase should be 200 to 500 FPM, and also keep an eye on your altimeter. Increasing your throttle further will maintain altitude, and reducing the throttle will continue your descent.

In the background, you will see the first contours of the airport runway and the landing lights. The medium-intensity approach lighting system (MALSR) has a row of flashing strobe lights that resemble tracer shells being fired at the runway, along with steadily burning roll guidance lights just before the runway. On the left of the runway, you will see the visual approach slope indicator (VASI) lights. Using two light bars, this indicator tells you whether you have selected the proper glide slope and altitude during your approach. If the bar at the back is red and the bar at the front is white, you are precisely on the correct glide path to the runway. If both bars are white, you are too high, and if both bars are red, you are too low.

Using the VASI and MALSR

Figure 13.3 shows the approach to Oakland Airport.

Preparing to Land

If the landing approach has gone according to plan, you should be on the correct glide path to the runway. Check your vertical speed

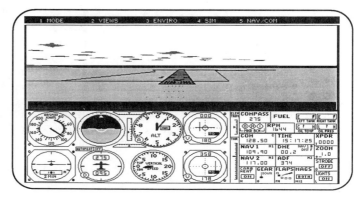

Figure 13.3: Oakland Airport

of 200 to 500 FPM again. If your descent speed is too high, increase the throttle. If the approach is too flat, or if you start climbing, decrease the throttle. You can make small corrections in the course heading by gently applying the ailerons.

Landing

As soon as you have flown beyond the threshold of the runway, pick your touchdown point and let the Cessna descend more. At 20 to 30 feet above the ground, level the plane by cautiously pulling the nose back while further reducing the throttle. In effect, you are trying to create a controlled stall onto the runway.

As the aircraft descends or flattens out in the final moments, gently keep the nose up and cut the engines. Keep the nose up until you see and hear the stall warning followed by the squeal of the wheels hitting the tarmac. Apply the brakes by repeatedly pressing the period (.) key until you have slowed to a reasonable taxi speed. Don't forget to retract your flaps. Figure 13.4 shows the screen as the plane lands.

Taxi to your parking position. Then switch off the carburetor heat, the landing lights, and the magnetos.

Figure 13.4: Landing on runway 27R

Steps to Descending and Landing Your Plane

Here is a summary of the key steps to a successful descent and touchdown.

Summary

1. Select the Oakland 27R—Landing Approach flight mode.
2. Call up ATIS on a COM radio frequency of 126.0 Mhz.
3. Perform a cross-check of instruments and indicators.
4. Calculate the rate of descent. (For this step, the rate of descent should be 700 to 800 FPM).
5. Start your descent by lowering the elevators (press the 8 key) and reducing the engine speed (press the 3 key).
6. Turn the carburetor heat and lights on (press the H and L keys).
7. Maintain a vertical speed of 700 to 800 FPM. Use the elevators to adjust vertical speed.
8. Maintain an engine speed of 1419 RPM (1499 RPM with the carburetor heat off).
9. Maintain a heading of 275 degrees. Use the ailerons to adjust the heading (press the 4 and 6 keys).

10. Maintain an airspeed of 95 to 100 knots.

11. Conduct a final check. (See the checklist in this step.)

12. Start your final landing approach ½ mile from the runway (as measured on the DME indicator).

13. Maintain an altimeter reading of 120 to 200 feet MSL. If you are too low, increase the throttle with the 9 key.

14. Reduce your vertical speed to 200 to 500 FPM by increasing the throttle. Don't use the elevators.

15. Maintain a landing speed of 80 to 90 knots.

16. Pick your touchdown point.

17. Flatten out your approach at 20 to 30 feet above the ground.

18. Cut the engine.

19. Slowly raise the elevators with the 2 key to stall the airplane.

20. Once you are on the ground, apply the brakes with the period (.) key.

21. Retract your flaps and switch off the carburetor heat, lights, and magnetos.

22. Pat yourself on the back.

Rectangular Traffic Pattern

You should now know the basics of flying. This step helps you refine these abilities by flying a basic rectangular traffic pattern.

The purpose of flying a traffic pattern is to practice takeoff, 90-degree turns, descent, and landing. Successfully completing this step shows that you have the flight savvy and coordination skills that are necessary to a good pilot and demonstrates that you can fly a flight from beginning to end.

Setting Your Position

To practice rectangular traffic patterns without danger, we will use La Guardia airport in New York City. You must move the plane to La Guardia. Use the Position Set command to quickly relocate your plane. Bring up the Nav/Com menu (menu 5) and select the Position Set option. Then enter the following values for the aircraft position (use number keys on the main keypad, not on the numeric keypad). Press the Enter key after each entry, and when you are finished, press the spacebar to return to the simulation.

North: 17091

East: 21026

Altitude: 22

Heading: 308

After you set these coordinates, your airplane is on the runway at La Guardia. If you press the Scroll Lock key followed by the 7 key to look out the left front window, you can very faintly see the twin spires of the World Trade Center. Return to the front view by pressing the Scroll Lock key followed by the 8 key.

Figure 14.1 shows the basic rectangular traffic pattern you will be flying. The figure includes a course headings chart.

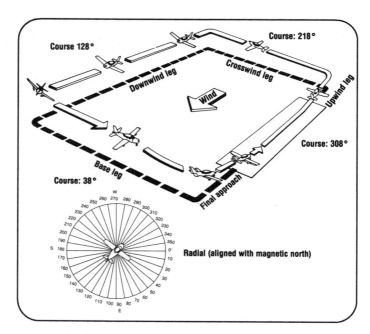

Figure 14.1: Basic rectangular traffic pattern with course headings chart

Preparing to Take Off

Before you take off to fly your rectangular traffic pattern, you must, of course, make your flight preparations, such as obtaining weather information, going through your takeoff checklist, and requesting takeoff clearance from the control tower. Flight simulator does not have an ATIS station for La Guardia, so to get weather information, tune into the nearby ATIS at JFK International Airport on a COM frequency of 119.10 Mhz.

Perform your checks conscientiously, as described in Step 9. These checks are for your own safety.

Once you have performed all the checks and have received clearance from the tower, increase the throttle to 881 RPM to begin taxiing down the runway. Check that the flaps are extended to the 10-degree position.

Taxiing

Taking Off

Align the aircraft with the center line of the runway. Slowly increase the throttle to full. At a speed of about 75 knots, the airplane should lift off the ground without any application of the elevator.

Once you have flown over the end of the runway, retract the landing gear. As no obstacles are expected, keep the Cessna ascending at the low rate of climb of 500 FPM. Use the elevators to adjust the rate of climb.

Flying the Upwind Leg

When the altimeter indicates an altitude of 1900 feet above mean sea level, retract the takeoff flaps. Reduce the throttle to a speed of 2077 RPM. Your directional gyro should read 308 degrees during this phase. Figure 14.2 shows the screen as you start flying the rectangular traffic pattern.

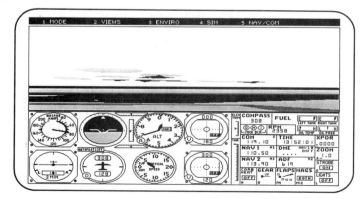

Figure 14.2: The beginning of the basic traffic pattern

Flying the Crosswind Leg

Continue to climb to 2100 feet. Then start a standard turn to the left. Look for the required 30-degree bank on the artificial horizon using the bank and turn indicator. If the aircraft is in the desired bank, the turn and bank indicator shows a turning speed of 3 degrees per second (the wing rolls onto the L mark).

If your turning speed is too slow or too fast, you can correct the bank by gently using the ailerons. Perform cross-checks regularly because the flight values change constantly. Be sure to monitor your altimeter and vertical speed indicator to ensure that you maintain your gradual climb of 500 FPM.

Ending the Turn

Heading: 218°

About 15 degrees before reaching your desired heading of 218 degrees, finish the turning maneuver by changing slowly from a bank to horizontal flight, applying the ailerons and the vertical rudder. At a course heading of 233 degrees, you must start ending the turn. During the crosswind leg, your final heading should be 218 degrees.

Flying the Downwind Leg

Heading: 128°

Shortly after you reach the altitude for the traffic pattern (2300 feet above MSL), start another left turn with a bank of 30 degrees. Start ending your turn at a heading of 143 degrees. At a heading of 128 degrees, bring the aircraft back to straight and level flight. Maintain this altitude for the traffic pattern. You are now on the downwind leg, parallel to the takeoff and landing runway. Your screen looks like Figure 14.3.

As soon as you can see the end of the runway from the left window, start your landing preparations according to visual flight rules. Switch on the carburetor heat and reduce the throttle to 1475 RPM. Extend the flaps to 10 degrees and lower the nose until you reach a descent speed of 500 FPM. Return to a front view out of your cockpit.

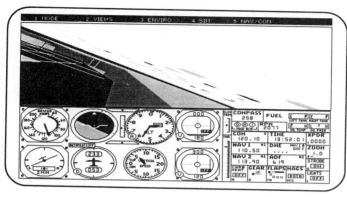

Figure 14.3: Flying a 30-degree turn

Flying the Base Leg

Out your left window you should see the contours of the La Guardia runway that you took off from. After you have flown beyond the end of the landing strip (as viewed sideways out your left window), return to the forward view out your cockpit window. You are now ready to turn left for the base leg. Start a standard turn to the left with a bank of 25 degrees, ending the turn 15 degrees before you reach a heading of 38 degrees. Keep to this heading and begin preparations for landing. Reduce the throttle to 1250 RPM to reach a final approach speed of 80 to 90 knots. Deploy your landing gear and observe your instruments to see that all is in order.

Heading 38°

Flying the Final Approach

The timing for your final turn is critical because you must accurately point the nose of your plane in the direction that the runway extends. If you undershoot or overshoot the turn, you will not be positioned correctly for the final landing approach. Peer out your left window, using the runway as a visual landmark. Just before the runway reaches the center of the window, switch back to a forward view and start a standard turn to the left. Come to a course

Heading:
308°

heading of 308 degrees, remembering to start ending the turn before you reach this heading (at a heading of 323 degrees). If necessary, correct your position by gently moving the ailerons. Figure 14.4 shows your plane as you make your final approach for landing.

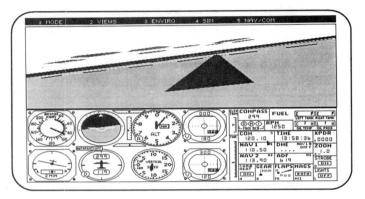

Figure 14.4: Final approach for landing

You now have a direct course to the runway, so do the following:

- Fully extend the flaps.
- Use a speed of descent of about 500 FPM. Adjust the throttle as necessary to maintain this speed.
- Lower the landing gear.
- Fly at a speed of 80 to 90 knots.

Touching
down

As soon as you have flown over the end of the runway, level off the plane and let it flatten out. If you are not satisfied with your performance, you can make a touch-and-go landing and try the maneuver again.

If you want to practice this mode many times, consider saving the mode to disk so that you need not reenter the position coordinates each time you restart Flight Simulator. To do this, enter your position coordinates for La Guardia. Then call up the Save Flight

Mode to Disk menu by pressing the ; key. Enter **La Guardia** as the title of the mode, press Enter, and save the mode to disk by pressing the 4 key on the main keypad. Call up this new mode from the mode library under the Mode pull-down menu.

Radio Navigation

This step explains Flight Simulator navigation and the use of navigational radios. You must understand flight navigation to travel from point A to point B by the shortest and safest path. Navigation can be divided into three categories: pilotage, dead reckoning, and VOR/ADF radio navigation.

To navigate the Flight Simulator world using radio beacons, you need to have the charts that show the locations and frequencies of all VOR and nondirectional beacon (NDB) stations. If you have the SubLOGIC scenery disks, you should already have these maps, but if you have only the Microsoft scenery disk, you must order them separately as they are supplementary materials.

Pilotage

Pilotage is the classic type of navigation. You mark your intended path on a map and orient yourself using visible landmarks such as rivers, expressways, railroad tracks, and large cities. However, pilotage is fraught with disadvantages and dangers. Usually, you cannot fly directly to your destination, because a flight is seldom a straight line when you fly using land-based points of orientation. For example, when you fly from Los Angeles to San Francisco, you can orient yourself using the coastline, but this is not the shortest or most direct path because of the curvature of the coast, Also, if the visual conditions deteriorate, or if you fly over large stretches of land or water without reference points, your ability to orient becomes limited or impossible. Thus, pilotage is a useful supplement to other forms of navigation, but you should not rely on it exclusively.

Orientation using visible landmarks

Dead Reckoning

Dead reckoning differs from pilotage in that you determine your position and flight path using computation. To determine the heading for your flight, you consider the factors of speed, time difference, distance, and wind effects. Dead reckoning used alone is not

Navigation using computation

very accurate, but when combined with pilotage, it becomes an effective method of navigation.

VOR and ADF Radio Navigation

The third and most accurate way of determining your position and course is to use VOR and ADF navigation, using ground-based radio beacons. Flight Simulator has two different types of radio beacons: the very high frequency omnidirectional range (VOR) beacon used with the Nav radios in conjunction with the OBI azimuth indicators, and the nondirectional radio beacon (NDB) used with the automatic direction finder (ADF) instrument.

Using the ADF

Finding the course toward the transmitter

Using the automatic direction finder (ADF), you can determine the direction to a nondirectional beacon (NDB) referenced to the longitudinal axis of the airplane. This direction is displayed on an indicator and shows you the bearing, relative to the nose of the aircraft, to the selected transmitter. Figure 15.1 shows an ADF display.

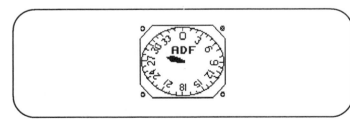

Figure 15.1: ADF display

Structure of the ADF

As described in Step 7, you can call up the ADF display instead of the OBI 2 azimuth display. The ADF instrument has a fixed 360-degree scale and a display needle. The structure and operation of the ADF display are similar to those of a compass, except that the zero-degree direction is always the direction of the plane's nose, regardless of the course heading.

Homing Method Using the ADF

The most common manner of approaching an NDB is the simple, straightforward homing method. After you set the frequency of the beacon on the ADF receiver, the needle of the compass points toward the selected transmitter. Turn the airplane in the direction of the ground station until the needle on the ADF indicator shows zero degrees, and you will be heading directly toward that station.

Disadvantages of the ADF

Unfortunately, Flight Simulator version 4.0 has only a few preprogrammed NDBs. Because of the paucity of NDB stations, navigation using the ADF is difficult. VOR navigation is simpler and more accurate because it is not subject to atmospheric interference and there are more VOR stations. In addition, using the DME indicator, you can also obtain distance and speed information relative to a VOR station.

Using VOR Navigation

Navigation using the VOR is usually used for short- to medium-distance flights. A VOR operates as follows: a sharply focused radio beam rotates at a constant rate. Every time the focused beam passes north, an omnidirectional beam is switched on briefly. The direction to the VOR can be calculated using the measured time between the focused beam and the omnidirectional beam together with the known rotation rate. If, say, 90 seconds passes between the omnidirectional pulse and the appearance of the rotating focused beam, and the beam is rotating clockwise at 1 degree per second, you are east (at 90 degrees) of the VOR station. Of course, the rotational speed of the focused beam is much faster than this, and the time that is measured between pulses is measured in mere fractions of a second.

How VOR navigation works

The phase difference between a reference signal (omnidirectional beam) and a circulating signal (focused beam) is determined by the radio navigation system on board the aircraft. This phase difference specifies the angle with respect to the VOR station and is shown on the OBI azimuth display.

The VOR guide beam radials

The guide beams transmitted by the VOR station form course lines, or radials, similar to the spokes of a wheel. The VOR on-board system can evaluate, and use for navigational purposes, 360 radials. The 0° radial is always aligned with magnetic north; and, reading clockwise around the radial circle, 90° is east, 180° is south and 270° is west.

Setting the NAV Receiver

Each VOR station has its own transmission frequency. You must set this frequency on the NAV receiver. The only limitation is that you must be located within the transmission range of the beacon. Step 7 describes how to set the NAV receiver. The maps or charts that you need for navigation show you the locations and frequencies of VOR stations in your area.

Using the OBI Azimuth Display

The azimuth display (Figure 15.2) has these components:

- course indicator/selector

- course deviation indicator (CDI) needle

- centering mark

- TO/FROM indicator

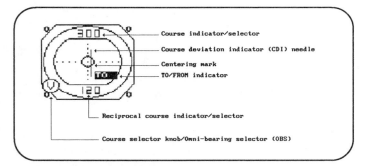

Figure 15.2: OBI azimuth display

- reciprocal course indicator/selector
- course selector knob/omnibearing selector (OBS)

Use the omnibearing selector knob to select the VOR radial that you want to intercept or fly on. You turn this knob by pressing the V key, followed by the 1 or 2 key (depending on whether you want OBI 1 or OBI 2) on the main keypad. Then press the + or − key on the main keypad to increase or decrease the course indicator until the CDI needle in the OBI is centered. To adjust the course indicator with the mouse, click the right or left side of the digits on the course selector, or click the course selector knob/omnibearing selector (OBS).

The course selector knob or omnibearing selector (OBS)

If the FROM indicator is on, with the CDI needle centered, the correct VOR radial appears in the upper course indicator. If the TO indicator is on, with the CDI needle centered, the correct VOR radial appears in the lower reciprocal course indicator.

Course and reciprocal course indicators

The Nav receiver calculates the VOR radial that you are currently following and displays, via the OBI's course deviation indicator needle, whether you are left or right of this VOR radial as compared to the course indicator heading you have chosen on the OBI. If the CDI needle is centered, you are crossing or are flying directly on the VOR radial that appears on either the course indicator or the reciprocal course indicator, depending on whether the FROM or TO indicator is on.

The course deviation indicator (CDI) needle

The TO/FROM indicator shows you whether you are on the radial displayed by the course indicator or on the radial 180 degrees opposite, displayed by the reciprocal course indicator. When *FROM* appears, the VOR radial you are currently following (assuming your course deviation needle is centered) appears in the top course indicator of the OBI. When *TO* appears, the current VOR radial appears in the reciprocal course indicator. The purpose of the TO/FROM indicator is to prevent disorientation as to the proper course to fly toward, or away from, a VOR station. Remember that when you fly toward a VOR station, the TO indicator should be on, and when you fly away from a VOR station, the FROM indicator should be on.

The TO/FROM indicator

Using Two VORs to Identify Your Position

Flight Simulator provides two Nav and corresponding OBIs so you can tune in different VOR stations simultaneously. Thus, you can pinpoint your position by plotting on the navigational maps the two VOR radials you are currently intersecting. The procedure is quite simple and is illustrated in Figure 15.3. Note that even though the plane appears headed toward the Seal Beach VOR, the FROM indicator is on. Ordinarily, when you fly toward a VOR station, the TO indicator should be on, but to avoid misreading the course indicators for your position, always make sure both FROM indicators are on. Reading the top course indicators on both OBIs gives you the proper VOR radials to plot. The plane's current position is at the intersection of the two VOR radials.

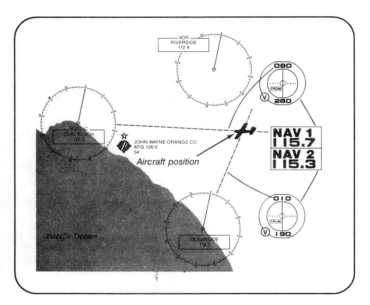

Figure 15.3: Using two VORs to identify position.

Step 16

ILS

The VOR/ADF radio navigation system discussed in Step 15 is used mainly for air-route navigation. The instrument landing system (ILS) described in this step is designed exclusively to help you safely make your final approach. You can also display the landing approach using the head-up display (HUD) window projection EFIS/CFPD system.

The instrument landing system has four main components:

- Localizer transmitter
- Glideslope transmitter
- Marker beacons
- Approach lights

The Localizer Transmitter

The localizer transmitter provides horizontal guidance, allowing the cockpit crew to make a direct landing approach even under poor weather conditions by aligning the plane horizontally with a VOR-like radial that is lined up with the runway. The localizer receiver in the plane can thus report whether the plane is to the left or right of the runway.

Horizontal guidance

The antennas of the localizer transmitter are 900 to 3000 feet beyond the end of the runway. They transmit a guide beam along the center line of the runway. You can usually receive the localizer transmission starting at a distance of 20 nautical miles from the runway.

The Glideslope Transmitter

The glideslope transmitter operates in a manner similar to that of the localizer transmitter, except that it provides vertical guidance information. The glideslope guidance beam is inclined, or sloped,

Vertical guidance

at an angle of 2 to 4 degrees from the ground and tells the pilot whether the plane is above or below the correct descent path. This glideslope ensures that the plane will descend at the proper rate, and that the altitude of the plane is correct.

The Glidepath

The horizontal guidance provided by the localizer transmitter and the vertical guidance supplied by the glideslope transmitter together make up the glidepath. If the aircraft is precisely on the glidepath, it will be on the optimum path to the runway.

Marker Beacons

In an ILS approach, the VHF radio marker beacons provide the pilot with information about the distance to the runway. There are three markers:

- Outer marker
- Middle marker
- Inner marker

Using the OMI indicator

When you fly over the outer marker, which is about 5 miles from the runway, an acoustical 400-Hz signal (two long beeps per second) sounds. At the same time, the blue O lamp on the OMI indicator lights. At a distance of 0.6 nautical miles before the runway, the yellow middle marker lamp comes on, and a 1300-Hz audio signal (a long beep followed by a short beep) sounds. (Flight Simulator 4.0 does not currently support the inner marker light.)

Figure 16.1 illustrates the marker system.

Approach Lights

The approach light system consists of the visual slope indicator (VASI), runway end identifier lights (REIL), and medium-intensity approach lighting system (MALSR). The VASI and

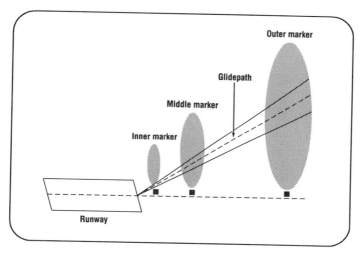

Figure 16.1: The marker beacons and glidepath

MALSR, described in Step 13, are essential for visual guidance during landing approaches. The REIL consists of two flashing lights positioned on both sides of the runway to help the pilot distinguish the runway from the surrounding terrain.

The ILS Reception System

Setting the ILS frequency

Only the OBI 1 azimuth display contains a glideslope indicator. Therefore, you can use only the Nav 1 receiver to tune in ILS stations. Set the radio frequency for the particular runway ILS station that you are approaching in the same way that you did for a VOR station. A list of runway ILS stations for each city appears in the appendix of this book.

Flying an ILS approach

During the landing approach, try to keep the point of intersection of the vertical and horizontal needles located at the center point of the OBI 1 azimuth display. When this happens, you are on the proper glidepath to the runway. Remember that the sensitivity of the needles is four times as great as for the VOR display.

If the horizontal needle is above the center position, the aircraft must gain altitude because it is beneath the glidepath. If the needle is below the center position, you must choose a steeper landing approach to return to the proper glidepath.

The vertical needle shows you the course deviation to the left or right of the glidepath. Correct your course by applying the ailerons.

EFIS/CFPD

Using the EFIS/ CFPD head-up display

The Flight Simulator EFIS/CFPD display provides an additional landing aid. The electronic flight instrument systems (EFIS) or command flight path display (CFPD) projects the glidepath to the runway on the windshield of the cockpit using rectangles, a "yellow brick road," or telephone poles.

To activate this display, you must first tune in the ILS station on the Nav 1 radio for the runway you want to use. Then select EFIS/ CFPD Display on the Nav/Com main menu. Enter the required parameters as described in Step 7.

Step 17

Slewing

This step describes how to use the Flight Simulator slewing controls. As mentioned in Step 2, slewing is a special nonflight mode that lets you move rapidly from point to point in the Flight Simulator world. Slewing lets you reposition your airplane visually, because in this mode you can see scenery out your cockpit windows. Slewing mode uses two types of movement: translation and rotation.

Slewing controls work only in slew mode, which you enter by selecting option 9 on the Nav/Com menu. You exit slew mode by again selecting option 9 on the Nav/Com menu.

Translation

Translation is the movement that occurs when you move your plane from one location to another. You can translate the aircraft right and left, backward and forward, and up and down from your present position using the translational slew keys (see Step 2 for a list of these keys). The top of your screen displays your north and east coordinates along with your altitude. To move slowly, press and hold down the direction key for a short time, and to move quickly, hold down the key for a longer time. With the mouse, you can translate forward or backward only by rolling the mouse (the mouse pointer must not be visible on screen) forward or backward, respectively. The left mouse button freezes all motion, and the right mouse button turns the mouse pointer on and off.

Rotation

Rotation refers to the revolving, or turning, movement that occurs around one of the plane's axes. Note that during rotation, the plane does not change position; only its attitude is altered. There are three axes of rotation, and thus three types of rotational slewing movement: yawing, rolling, and pitching. Yawing involves rotation about the aircraft's vertical axis. Yawing changes the plane's heading. Rolling involves rotation about the aircraft's longitudinal axis. Rolling makes the plane's wings bank left or right. Pitching involves rotation about the aircraft's lateral axis. Pitching moves the plane's nose up or down. Figure 17.1 shows the three types of slewing rotation.

See Step 2 for a list of the keys that control slewing rotation. For rotation, the mouse can control only yawing movement: this is accomplished by moving the mouse right or left (the mouse pointer must not be visible on screen). Again, the left mouse button freezes all motion while the right mouse button turns the mouse pointer on and off.

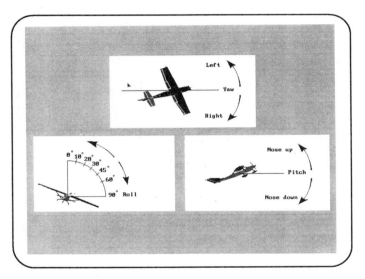

Figure 17.1: Slewing rotation about three axes: yaw, roll, and pitch

Entertainment

Once you have mastered the basics of flying, you are ready to try some of Flight Simulator's entertainment features. You will find these listed under the Entertainment option in the Mode menu.

Multiplayer Mode

Flight Simulator can link another player into the simulation using a second computer and a serial port connection. Connect the two computers directly with a null modem cable or, alternatively, a telephone using a regular modem connected to one of your Com ports.

Setting the Communications Parameters

You must set the following Multiplayer menu options (Figure 18.1) on both computers. Use option A on the Multiplayer menu to tell Flight Simulator which serial port to use. Com 1 to 4 ports are available. Set the data transmission rate (baud rate) using menu option B. Make sure to select the same baud rate for both computers. For the baud rate, you should use the maximum transmission rate of the available hardware. With modems, you will usually set the baud rate to 300, 1200, or 2400, depending on the rate your modem can handle.

Establishing Modem Connections

After you specify the communications protocol—the Com port and the baud rate—make the connection between two Hayes-compatible modems. To do this, one player first dials the other player using menu option 4, Dial. To dial, enter the telephone number of the other player in the message box that appears at the bottom of the screen and then confirm the entry with the Enter key. If the other player has selected menu option 5, Wait for Ring, the computer receives the call automatically. As soon as the connection is made, the connect message appears in the message box, and the computers are now ready to exchange data. When both

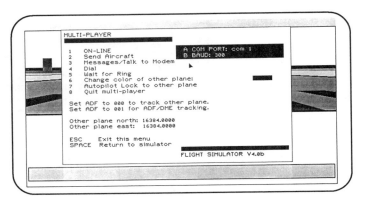

Figure 18.1: Multiplayer setup menu

players have selected the ON-LINE menu option 1, data exchange actually starts. The computers exchange the coordinates of the airplanes (position, altitude, and speed) continuously from now on.

Establishing Direct Cable Connections

The fastest and easiest method of exchanging flight data is the direct connection of two computers using a null modem cable connected between the serial ports. To do this, again enter the baud rate and the selected port of your computer on the Multiplayer menu. Then start data exchange by using the ON-LINE menu option.

Sending Messages to the Other Player

To send a message to the other player, call up a text window with the Messages/Talk to Modem menu option. Enter the message and send it by pressing the Return key. When flying, you can directly return to message mode by pressing the O key on the main keypad.

Using Multiplayer Utilities

You can automatically lock the autopilot to the other plane by selecting menu item 7. If both aircraft are at the same altitude, turn off your engine and then start following the other plane. You can also use the ADF display to locate the other player. Set the ADF receiver to 000. The pointer of the ADF instrument now points in the direction of the other airplane. (You must, of course, turn on your ADF instrument from the Nav/Com menu.)

Ending Multiplayer Mode

To quit Multiplayer mode, use option 8, Quit Multiplayer. You will exit the menu and return to the original flight mode.

Crop Dusting

The Crop Duster option activates the following game. On board a crop duster, you are to spray a field with insecticide as quickly as possible. You are on the runway of a small airport and ready for takeoff. To help you navigate, you can switch on the map window and fly in a northerly direction toward the first row of the field. The field is divided into 64 squares. A high fence runs part way around the field. For this reason, maintain an altitude of about 50 feet over the field, but climb to at least 150 feet when flying over the edge of the field. As soon as you have flown over the edge of the field, switch the spraying system on or off with the I key. Use the spray very sparingly to achieve a higher point score.

To end spraying, press Esc or land the airplane. You will then be scored on coverage, amount of overspray, and elapsed time. For every section of the field that you spray, you receive 10 points. When the spraying system is switched on, you lose one point per second. You have a total of 500 seconds to spray the entire field. When this time runs out, the plane crashes, or you end play, the program displays a table showing the final point score, the number of field squares dusted, and the elapsed time. Exit Crop Duster by selecting Normal Flight or another entertainment option.

Scoring

Formation Flying

The Formation Flying option lets you follow a second airplane. You attempt to follow a computer-generated aircraft in one of the

Following another plane

seven different flight modes that you can select. The flight maneuvers of the leading plane, some of which are quite reckless, require experience and practice with Flight Simulator. The smoke trail that marks the course of the other aircraft helps you follow it. However, even the first of the seven flight modes requires all your skills to fly an obstacle course through San Francisco. You fly over the Golden Gate Bridge into the center of San Francisco and follow the white smoke trail of the other airplane. You can also tour other cities, such as Manhattan and Chicago, or you can buzz a World War I hanger. Bridges, walls, and towers form the backdrop for joint aerobatics in two other menu options. You also can fly off the coast of Southern California near San Diego and attempt to land on the aircraft carrier Nimitz anchored there.

EFIS/CFPD

The EFIS/CFPD Entertainment menu gives you a choice of flying four different ILS landing scenarios using the front window navigational projection system. You can choose among a calm ILS landing at San Francisco, a stormy ILS approach to Oakland, a thunderstorm ILS approach to Champaign (Illinois), and a Learjet cruise to Chicago's O'Hare International Airport.

World War I Ace

The World War I option lets you prove your flying capabilities. The World War I Ace game requires quick reaction to find enemy attackers and safely control the aircraft in extreme situations. Start on runway 27 and keep heading in an easterly direction. After flying over the border river, declare war using the W key. Now you must carefully observe the airspace using the radar window. If an enemy airplane closes in on you, defend against the attack with the machine guns (press the spacebar). You can also destroy enemy ground targets by dropping a bomb, using the X key. Keep a close eye on the fuel gauge, oil pressure, oil temperature, and other important instruments during the flight. If these instruments show the slightest change, return to base immediately; you may have sustained damage.

The aim of the World War I game is to collect as many points as possible by destroying factories (4 points), fuel depots (2 points), or airplanes (1 point). Figure 18.2 shows a war report, or score, screen.

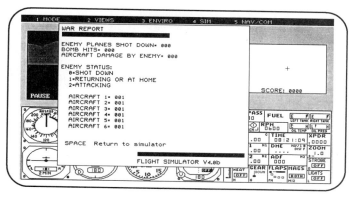

Figure 18.2: War Report

Sailplane & Learjet

This step describes soaring with the Schweizer 2-32 sailplane and flying the Gates Learjet 25G.

Flying the Sailplane

The sailplane you will use is a two-seat glider with a wing span of 57 feet, a length of about 26.75 feet, a glide ratio of 34 to 1, and a maximum speed of 130 knots. The sailplane comes with elevators, ailerons, and rudders just like the Cessna, but it has dive brakes in place of flap controls.

Soaring Basics

Because a sailplane is not moved forward by a propeller or jet engine, it must make use of the property of gliding. For this to work, the upward motion of the surrounding air must be greater than the rate of descent of the sailplane. This relationship allows the aircraft to maintain altitude or, in the best cases, even climb. To achieve the proper conditions, you need to find areas with mountains or warm air masses with sufficient rising air. Such thermal currents make safe soaring possible.

Ridge Soaring

On the Mode main menu, select Sailplane-Ridge Soaring. Now you can soar along the side of Mt. Tamalpais with a reduced instrument cluster (Figure 19.1).

Take advantage of thermal wind currents that are deflected upward and thus create lift. Do not turn toward the mountainside, but rather toward the valley in long, drawn-out figure eights. In doing so, fly through descent areas with sufficient altitude and through ascent areas with reduced speed. Try to climb to the altitude of the mountain top, because you achieve the best climbing performance there. Do not fly over the top of the mountain under

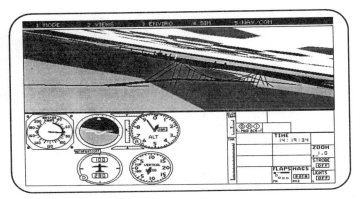

Figure 19.1: Flying the thermal currents on the side of Mt.Tamalpais

any circumstances. The air on the leeward side of the mountain descends due to adiabatic heating and drying. Turbulence also may form here.

You need to return with sufficient altitude to the airport on the other side of the ridge near the ocean. Never forget that you cannot use engine power to compensate for an imminent loss in altitude.

Flying the landing approach

You have an optimal glide angle for the landing approach if you are descending at 500 FPM. Make corrections by extending or retracting the dive brakes, using the same function keys you use to control the flaps. At about 50 feet above the ground, start to level off the sailplane by pulling up gently. Bring the plane into a straight and level position and then flatten out the plane.

Thermal Soaring

Gaining altitude

As an alternative to soaring along the ridge, you can select the Thermal Soaring option on the Mode menu. Ground heating causes thermal up-currents to form. Thus, you will notice an increase in the vertical velocity indicator when you fly over a brown field. Rising air masses (thermals) are created because brown fields and desert areas reflect more of the sunlight than they absorb, whereas forests and green fields absorb more heat than they reflect. You must wait for the right moment when the thermal current raises one of the wings. As soon as you notice the wing tip rising, begin a turn. Use these up-currents to gain altitude quickly with circular maneuvers. Climb with a bank of about 30 degrees. When starting the turn, use the ailerons and vertical rudder to achieve the desired bank. Because banking the aircraft decreases the lift, you must somewhat increase the speed. As soon as you reach the desired bank, neutralize the ailerons and when you have gained enough altitude, level off the sailplane. If you need to gain more altitude, keep circling over the brown field. Figure 19.2 shows the screen during thermal soaring.

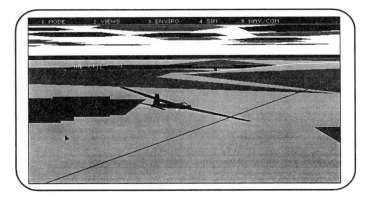

Figure 19.2: Thermal soaring

Substituting the Sailplane for a Motorized Aircraft

You can also fly the sailplane in any other area instead of using the Cessna or the jet. Remember, however, that you must start the sailplane with sufficient altitude; it cannot be started from the ground.

Flying the Learjet

The Gates Learjet 25G is a streamlined twin-turbojet-powered aircraft. You can cruise at altitudes up to 51,000 feet at speeds up to 464 knots. The Learjet seats 10 people and has a maximum take-off weight of 16,200 pounds, so flying it requires a lighter, slower, and steadier touch than flying the Cessna. The Learjet won't respond as quickly as the Cessna or the sailplane because of its weight and inertia, but it is much faster and will enable you to travel farther and faster.

However, because of the jet's two very powerful turbojets, you can easily exceed the maximum safe operating speed. When this happens, the overspeed warning system sounds and displays a warning on your windshield, telling you that you must immediately reduce speed. If you continue to let the airplane get faster, supersonic shock waves will disable your ailerons and cause the airplane to go out of control. To recover from this situation, reduce power, pull up the nose, and if necessary, lower the landing gear to increase drag. Figure 19.3 shows the Learjet specifications.

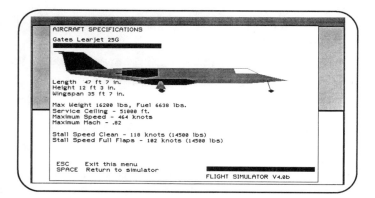

Figure 19.3: Learjet specifications

Learjet Instruments

Several changes occur in the instrument panel when you select the Learjet. Because the plane is powered by jet turbine engines and not a piston engine as with the Cessna, engine speed is measured on the tachometer as a percentage of full RPM rather than absolute RPM. The airspeed indicator is recalibrated to read speeds up to 550 knots and shows true airspeed rather than indicated airspeed. True airspeed is a more accurate measure of speed for fast aircraft because indicated airspeed depends on air pressure and can give false results at higher speeds and altitudes. If you have selected either EGA display driver option H or VGA display option M in your program setup, three other instruments also change. The vertical speed indicator is recalibrated to read speeds up to 8000 feet per minute. The Carb Heat control becomes the Spoilers control, and the Mags control changes to the Engs control. Spoilers increase drag and decrease lift and are activated by pressing the H key. The Engs control allows you to turn your engines on and off individually.

Step 20

Barnstorming

In this step you will take off from Oakland Airport and barnstorm under both the Golden Gate Bridge and the Bay Bridge, taking in the breathtaking scenery of the San Francisco Bay Area. The scenery for this area is especially detailed and impressive, for not only do you get glimpses of the two bridges and the bay, but you also can see downtown San Francisco, Treasure Island, the infamous Alcatraz Prison, and nearby Mt. Tamalpais in Marin and Mt. Sutro in San Francisco.

Getting Started

From the Mode menu, select the Oakland 27R Takeoff flight mode under menu option B. Press the spacebar to return to the cockpit, and you should have a clear view down Oakland's 27R runway. If it is nighttime, adjust your clock on the instrument panel to a daytime hour.

Making Flight Preparations

One absolutely essential navigation rule for flights is to establish a flight plan. For long flights, this plan provides information about the flight path, altitude, projected speed, and transmitting frequencies of VOR stations along the way. Because you will be flying only a short local flight in the Bay Area, you will mainly rely on visual landmarks and your directional gyro for navigation. On the barnstorming leg of the flight, you must never exceed an altitude of 250 feet; otherwise, you might slam into the decks or cabling of the bridges. The optimum altitude is 200 feet MSL to allow for minor fluctuations in altitude.

The trip itinerary is as follows: fly under the suspension portion of the Bay Bridge. After reaching Alcatraz Island, turn to a course heading of 242° and fly under the Golden Gate Bridge. After flying out the Golden Gate, you will double back toward San Francisco, taking in the sights along the way. You will return to

Your itinerary

Oakland, but this time you will land on Oakland South Field runway 11 on a course heading of 113°. Throughout the flight, you must watch your altimeter closely to keep from flying too high or low.

Taking Off

Course heading: 275°

First tune in the Oakland VOR station on the NAV 1 radio at 116.80 Mhz. Set the flaps to 10° and tune in the Oakland North Field ATIS on a COM frequency of 126.00 Mhz for an updated weather report. Go through the takeoff checklist (see Step 9). When you are ready, increase the throttle to maximum. At a speed of 75 knots, the Cessna will lift off by itself. Once you are clear of the runway, retract the landing gear and the flaps and reduce the throttle to 1724 RPM. Apply your elevators to bring the airplane out of its climb, but fine-tune the vertical speed to 0 FPM by using the elevator trim control. At the end of this phase, you should be on a course heading of 275° with an altitude of 200 feet.

Barnstorming the Bay Bridge

Course heading: 310°

When your DME indicator shows that you are 7 miles from the Oakland VOR station, make a slow right turn to a course heading of 310°. The Bay Bridge will appear directly in front of you. Keep your altitude below 250 feet and fly under the deck of the Bay Bridge. Glance out your left front window (press the Scroll Lock and 7 keys) and your left side window (press the Scroll Lock and 4 keys) to get a bird's-eye view of downtown San Francisco, the wharf area, and Alcatraz Island. In the distance you can see the twin red towers of the Golden Gate Bridge and the lush green slopes of Marin's Mt. Tamalpais.

Barnstorming the Golden Gate Bridge

Course heading: 242°

Return to a front view out your window by pressing the Scroll Lock and 8 keys. Using Alcatraz Island as a visual landmark, turn the plane left so that you are flying directly toward it (Alcatraz prison is the square white building perched on the green island just off San Francisco's Fisherman's Wharf). After passing directly over Alcatraz Island, bank the plane left until you reach a course heading of 242°. Then fly straight toward the Golden Gate Bridge. Keep your altitude below 250 feet to clear the deck of the bridge. Use the elevator trim to make small adjustments in nose pitch. Figure 20.1 shows your view.

Returning Home

To better orient yourself, call up the map window with the Num-Lock key. Change the scale of the map section with the + or − key on the main keypad. On your left is the San Francisco Peninsula, and on your right is Marin. You have completed the bridge portion of your flight, so you can now gain some altitude for the return leg. Turn the plane left and slightly raise the nose until you reach a course heading of 70° and an altitude of 500 feet. Pass over San Francisco and approach the bay.

Course heading: 70°

Setting the VOR Heading

You will use the OBI indicator to find the correct direction back to Oakland. Set the OBI 1 indicator by pressing the V key followed by the + or − key to adjust the course selector until the vertical CDI needle is centered and the TO indicator is on. The top course reading is the course heading you must follow to get back to

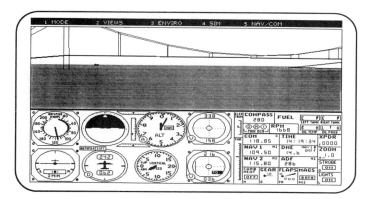

Figure 20.1: Golden Gate Bridge flyby

Oakland, so bring the plane about until your course heading on the directional gyro is the same as that on the OBI 1. At about 3.5 miles from the VOR station (as displayed on the DME), switch off the map (press NumLock twice) and look for the tracer strobe lights of runway 11 on the edge of the bay.

Landing

Course heading: 113°

Follow the descent and landing procedures outlined in Step 13. Make sure that the landing gear is extended, the flaps are set at 10°, and the throttle is reduced to 1419 RPM with the carburetor heat on. Align the plane with the tracer strobe lights so that the lights seem to be firing away from you vertically into the runway from the center of your screen. If you are positioned correctly, you should be on a course heading of 113°. Keep your vertical speed below 500 FPM for the touchdown.

Appendix

Airport Directory

New York and Boston Area

City: Airport	North	East	Alt.	Fuel	ILS (Rwy./Freq.)	ATIS (Freq.)
Block Island State:						
Block Island State	17352	21749	105	•		123.00
Boston:						
Logan Intl.	17899	21853	20	•		119.10
Bridgeport :						
Igor I. Sikorsky Memorial	17287	21249	10	•		120.90
Chester:						
Chester	17404	21434	416			
Danbury:						
Danbury Municipal	17360	21120	457			
Danielson:						
Danielson	17617	21607	239			
Farmingdale:						
Republic	17089	21177	81			
Hartford:						
Hartford-Brainard	17551	21371	19			
Islip:						
Long Island MacArthur	17132	21278	99			
Martha's Vineyard:						
Martha's Vineyard	17490	22043	68	•	24/108.7	121.40
Meriden:						
Meriden Markham Municipal	17447	21327	102			
New Haven:						
Tweed-New Haven	17339	21322	13			
New York:						
John F. Kennedy Intl.	17034	21065	12	•		119.10
New York:						
LaGuardia	17091	21026	22			
Oxford:						
Waterbury-Oxford	17422	21229	727			
Southbridge:						
Southbridge Municipal	17733	21543	697			
White Plains:						
Westchester Co.	17226	21065	439			
Willimantic:						
Windham	17573	21521	246			
Windsor Locks:						
Bradley Intl.	17638	21351	174			

Chicago Area

City: Airport	North	East	Alt.	Fuel	ILS (Rwy./Freq.)	ATIS (Freq.)
Aurora:						
Aurora Municipal	17152	16393	706			
Bloomington:						
Bloomington-Normal	16593	16246	875			
Champaign/Urbana:						
University of Illinois, Willard	16400	16465	754	•	32L/109.1	124.85
Chicago:						
Chicago-Midway	17156	16628	619	•		128.05
Chicago:						
Chicago-O'Hare Intl.	17243	16578	667	•	4L/111.3	135.15
					4R/110.1	
					9L/110.5	
					9R/111.1	
					14L/110.9	
					14R/109.7	
					22L/110.1	
					22R/111.3	
					27L/111.1	
					27R/110.5	
					32L/109.1	
					32R/110.7	
Chicago:						
Lansing Municipal	17052	16697	614			
Chicago:						
Meigs	17189	16671	592	•		
Chicago/Blue Island:						
Howel	17100	16627	600			
Chicago/Schaumburg Air:						
Schaumburg Air Park	17247	16515	795			
Chicago/West Chicago:						
DuPage	17213	16466	757			
Danville:						
Vermilion Co.	16471	16685	695			
Dwight:						
Dwight	16874	16404	630			
Frankfort:						
Frankfort	17025	16596	775			
Gibson City:						
Gibson City Municipal	16594	16461	759			
Joliet:						
Joliet Park District	17038	16490	582			
Kankakee:						
Greater Kankakee	16846	16597	625	•		123.00

City: Airport	North	East	Alt.	Fuel	ILS (Rwy./Freq.)	ATIS (Freq.)
Monee:						
Sanger	16980	16646	786			
Morris:						
Morris Municipal	17004	16413	588			
New Lenox:						
New Lenox-Howell	17025	16571	745			
Paxton:						
Paxton	16578	16507	780			
Plainfield:						
Clow Intl.	17116	16502	670			
Romeoville:						
Lewis University	17081	16518	672			
Urbana:						
Frasca Field	16446	16488	735			

Los Angeles Area

City: Airport	North	East	Alt.	Fuel	ILS (Rwy./Freq.)	ATIS (Freq.)
Avalon:						
Catalina (pvt.)	15149	5744	1602	•		122.70
Carlsbad:						
McClennan-Palomar	14931	6112	328			
Chino:						
Chino	15319	6079	650			
Compton:						
Compton	15334	5859	97			
Corona:						
Corona Municipal	15280	6083	533			
El Monte:						
El Monte	15397	5952	296			
Fallbrook:						
Fallbrook Community Airpark	15023	6144	708			
Hawthorne:						
Hawthorne Municipal	15358	5831	63			
Huntington Beach:						
Meadowlark	15244	5911	28			
LaVerne:						
Brackett Fld.	15378	6038	1011			
Los Angeles:						
Hughes (pvt.)	15386	5808	22	•		132.40

City: Airport	North	East	Alt.	Fuel	ILS (Rwy./Freq.)	ATIS (Freq.)
Los Angeles:						
Los Angeles Intl.	15374	5805	126	•		133.80
Oceanside:						
Oceanside Municipal	14974	6095	28			
Ontario:						
Ontario Intl.	15347	6099	952			
Riverside:						
Riverside Municipal	15288	6141	816			
San Diego:						
San Diego Intl.–						
Lindbergh Fl.	14761	6102	15	•		134.80
Santa Ana:						
John Wayne Airport						
(Orange Co.)	15211	5961	54	•		126.0
Santa Monica:						
Santa Monica Municipal	15402	5799	175	•		119.15
Torrance:						
Torrance Municipal	15308	5815	101			
Van Nuys:						
Van Nuys	15498	5811	799	•	16R/111.3	118.45

San Francisco Area

City: Airport	North	East	Alt.	Fuel	ILS (Rwy./Freq.)	ATIS (Freq.)
Antioch:						
Antioch	17406	5297	190			
Chico:						
Chico	18158	5567	239			
Columbia:						
Columbia	17269	5753	2116			
Concord:						
Buchanan	17452	5217	23			124.70
Crows Landing:						
NALF Crows Landing	17256	5370	200	•		
Fremont:						
(Sky sailing)	17224	5178	9			
Fresno:						
Chandler Downtown	16671	5752	279			
Fresno:						
Fresno Air Terminal	16679	5795	331			
Garberville:						
Garberville	18514	5010	544			

City: Airport	North	East	Alt.	Fuel	ILS (Rwy./Freq.)	ATIS (Freq.)
Hayward:						
Hayward	17328	5146	9			
Little River:						
Mendocino Co.	18174	4895	571			
Livermore:						
Livermore	17303	5251	397		25/110.5	
Lodi:						
Kingdon	17408	5460	16			
Lodi:						
Lodi	17447	5503	59			
Marysville:						
Yuba Co.	17840	5550	62			
Merced:						
Merced	16980	5608	154			
Minden:						
Douglas Co.	17584	6104	4717			
Modesto:						
Modesto City	17172	5518	98			
Monterey Peninsula:						
Monterey Peninsula	16862	5069	243			
Mountain View:						
NAS Moffett Fld.	17220	5133	9			
Novato:						
Hamilton	17532	5083	9			
Oakland S:						
Metro Oakland Intl.						
South Field	17363	5129	13	•	11/111.9	128.5
					29/108.7	
Oakland N:						
North Field						
(general aviation)	17355	5123	13	•	27R/109.9	126.0
Oakland:						
NAS Alameda	17404	5101	16			
Oroville:						
Oroville	18003	5592	200			
Palo Alto:						
Palo Alto	17243	5120	9			
Placerville:						
Placerville	17591	5748	2585			
Red Bluff:						
Red Bluff	18347	5500	348			
Reno:						
Cannon	17788	6176	4412			
Reno:						
Stead	17875	6169	5045			

City: Airport	North	East	Alt.	Fuel	ILS (Rwy./Freq.)	ATIS (Freq.)
Sacramento:						
Sacramento Metro	17681	5477	23			
Sacramento:						
Sacramento Exec.	17595	5482	23			
Salinas:						
Salinas	16856	5161	85			
San Carlos:						
San Carlos	17278	5085	9			
San Francisco:						
San Francisco Intl.	17340	5061	10	•	19L/108.9 28L/109.5 28R/111.7	118.85
San Jose:						
Reid-Hillview	17157	5195	134			
San Jose:						
San Jose	17184	5165	62	•	12R/111.10	125.2
Santa Rosa:						
Sonoma Co.	17756	5066	125			
Santa Rosa:						
Santa Rosa	17711	5066	98			
South Lake Tahoe:						
Lake Tahoe	17570	6016	6265			
Stockton:						
Stockton Metro	17312	5467	30			
Truckee-Tahoe:						
Truckee-Tahoe	17761	6031	5901			
Visalia:						
Visalia	16454	5831	292			
Watsonville:						
Watsonville	16995	5138	161			
Willows:						
Glenn Co.	18087	5409	138			

Seattle Area

City: Airport	North	East	Alt.	Fuel	ILS (Rwy./Freq.)	ATIS (Freq.)
Alderwood Manor:						
Martha Lake	21502	6670	500			
Arlington:						
Arlington Municipal	21616	6737	137			
Auburn:						
Auburn Municipal	21290	6586	57			

City: Airport	North	East	Alt.	Fuel	ILS (Rwy./Freq.)	ATIS (Freq.)
Bremerton:						
Bremerton National	21407	6470	481			
Everett:						
Snohomish Co. (Paine Field)	21525	6665	603	•	16/109.3	128.65
Issaquah:						
Issaquah	21362	6668	500			
Monroe:						
Flying F. Ranch	21481	6738	50			
Olympia:						
Olympia	21218	6343	206	•		124.40
Puyallup:						
Pierce Co.-Thun Fld.	21206	6534	530			
Port Angeles:						
William R. Fairchild Intl	21740	6375	288	•		122.80
Port Orchard:						
Port Orchard	21373	6483	370			
Renton:						
Renton Municipal	21351	6612	29			
Seattle:						
Boeing Fld./King Co. Intl.	21376	6596	17	•		127.75
Seattle:						
Seattle-Tacoma Intl.	21343	6584	429	•		118.00
Shelton:						
Sanderson Fld.	21353	6316	278			
Snohomish Co.:						
See Everett						
Snohomish:						
Harvey Fld.	21505	6711	16			
Spanaway:						
Shady Acres	21201	6501	425			
Spanaway:						
Spanaway	21215	6491	385			
Tacoma:						
Tacoma Narrows	21300	6480	292			

Index

Selections from The SYBEX Library

OPERATING SYSTEMS

The ABC's of DOS 4
Alan R. Miller
275pp. Ref. 583-2

This step-by-step introduction to using DOS 4 is written especially for beginners. Filled with simple examples, *The ABC's of DOS 4* covers the basics of hardware, software, disks, the system editor EDLIN, DOS commands, and more.

The ABC's of DOS 5
Alan Miller
267pp. Ref. 770-3

This straightforward guide will haven even first-time computer users working comfortably with DOS 5 in no time. Step-by-step lessons lead users from switching on the PC, through exploring the DOS Shell, working with directories and files, using essential commands, customizing the system, and trouble shooting. Includes a tear-out quick reference card and function key template.

ABC's of MS-DOS (Second Edition)
Alan R. Miller
233pp. Ref. 493-3

This handy guide to MS-DOS is all many PC users need to manage their computer files, organize floppy and hard disks, use EDLIN, and keep their computers organized. Additional information is given about utilities like Sidekick, and there is a DOS command and program summary. The second edition is fully updated for Version 3.3.

The ABC's of SCO UNIX
Tom Cuthbertson
263pp. Re. 715-0

A guide especially for beginners who want to get to work fast. Includes hands-on tutorials on logging in and out; creating and editing files; using electronic mail; organizing files into directories; printing; text formatting; and more.

The ABC's of Windows 3.0
Kris Jamsa
327pp. Ref. 760-6

A user-friendly introduction to the essentials of Windows 3.0. Presented in 64 short lessons. Beginners start with lesson one, while more advanced readers can skip ahead. Learn to use File Manager, the accessory programs, customization features, Program Manager, and more.

DESQview Instant Reference
Paul J. Perry
175pp. Ref. 809-2

This complete quick-reference command guide covers version 2.3 and DESQview 386, as well as QEMM (for managing expanded memory) and Manifest Memory Analyzer. Concise, alphabetized entries provide exact syntax, options, usage, and brief examples for every command. A handy source for on-the-job reminders and tips.

DOS 3.3 On-Line Advisor Version 1.1
SYBAR, Software Division of SYBEX, Inc.
Ref. 933-1

The answer to all your DOS problems. The DOS On-Line Advisor is an on-screen reference that explains over 200 DOS error messages. 2300 other citations cover all you ever needed to know about DOS. The DOS On-Line Advisor pops up on top of your working program to give you quick, easy help when you need it, and disappears when you don't. Covers thru version 3.3. Software package comes with 3½" and 5¼" disks. **System Requirements:** IBM compatible with DOS 2.0 or higher, runs with Windows 3.0, uses 90K of RAM.

DOS Instant Reference
SYBEX Prompter Series
Greg Harvey
Kay Yarborough Nelson
220pp. Ref. 477-1

A complete fingertip reference for fast, easy on-line help:command summaries, syntax, usage and error messages. Organized by function—system commands, file commands, disk management, directories, batch files, I/O, networking, programming, and more. Through Version 3.3.

DOS 5 Instant Reference
Robert M. Thomas
200pp. Ref. 804-1

The comprehensive quick guide to DOS—all its features, commands, options, and versions—now including DOS 5, with the new graphical interface. Concise, alphabetized command entries provide exact syntax, options, usage, brief examples, and applicable version numbers. Fully cross-referenced; ideal for quick review or on-the-job reference.

The DOS 5 User's Handbook
Gary Masters
Richard Allen King
400pp. Ref. 777-0

This is the DOS 5 book for users who are already familiar with an earlier version of DOS. Part I is a quick, friendly guide to new features; topics include the graphical interface, new and enhanced commands, and much more. Part II is a complete DOS 5 quick reference, with command summaries, in-depth explanations, and examples.

Encyclopedia DOS
Judd Robbins
1030pp. Ref. 699-5

A comprehensive reference and user's guide to all versions of DOS through 4.0. Offers complete information on every DOS command, with all possible switches and parameters—plus examples of effective usage. An invaluable tool.

Essential OS/2
(Second Edition)
Judd Robbins
445pp. Ref. 609-X

Written by an OS/2 expert, this is the guide to the powerful new resources of the OS/2 operating system standard edition 1.1 with presentation manager. Robbins introduces the standard edition, and details multitasking under OS/2, and the range of commands for installing, starting up, configuring, and running applications. For Version 1.1 Standard Edition.

Essential PC-DOS
(Second Edition)
Myril Clement Shaw
Susan Soltis Shaw
332pp. Ref. 413-5

An authoritative guide to PC-DOS, including version 3.2. Designed to make experts out of beginners, it explores everything from disk management to batch file programming. Includes an 85-page command summary. Through Version 3.2.

Graphics Programming
Under Windows
Brian Myers
Chris Doner
646pp. Ref. 448-8

Straightforward discussion, abundant examples, and a concise reference guide to graphics commands make this book a must for Windows programmers. Topics range from how Windows works to programming for business, animation, CAD, and desktop publishing. For Version 2.

Hard Disk Instant Reference
SYBEX Prompter Series
Judd Robbins
256pp. Ref. 587-5

Compact yet comprehensive, this pocket-sized reference presents the essential information on DOS commands used in managing directories and files, and in optimizing disk configuration. Includes a survey of third-party utility capabilities. Through DOS 4.0.

Inside DOS: A Programmer's Guide
Michael J. Young
490pp. Ref. 710-X

A collection of practical techniques (with source code listings) designed to help you take advantage of the rich resources intrinsic to MS-DOS machines. Designed for the experienced programmer with a basic understanding of C and 8086 assembly language, and DOS fundamentals.

Mastering DOS (Second Edition)
Judd Robbins
722pp. Ref. 555-7

"The most useful DOS book." This seven-part, in-depth tutorial addresses the needs of users at all levels. Topics range from running applications, to managing files and directories, configuring the system, batch file programming, and techniques for system developers. Through Version 4.

Mastering DOS 5
Judd Robbins
800pp. Ref.767-3

"The DOS reference to keep next to your computer," according to PC Week, this highly acclaimed text is now revised and expanded for DOS 5. Comprehensive tutorials cover everything from first steps for beginners, to advanced tools for systems developers—with emphasis on the new graphics interface. Includes tips, tricks, and a tear-out quick reference card and function key template.

Mastering SunOS
Brent D. Heslop
David Angell
588pp. Ref. 683-9

Learn to configure and manage your system; use essential commands; manage files; perform editing, formatting, and printing tasks; master E-mail and external communication; and use the SunView and new Open Window graphic interfaces.

Mastering Windows 3.0
Robert Cowart
592pp. Ref.458-5

Every Windows user will find valuable how-to and reference information here.

With full details on the desktop utilities; manipulating files; running applications (including non-Windows programs); sharing data between DOS, OS/2, and Windows; hardware and software efficiency tips; and more.

Understanding DOS 3.3
Judd Robbins
678pp. Ref. 648-0

This best selling, in-depth tutorial addresses the needs of users at all levels with many examples and hands-on exercises. Robbins discusses the fundamentals of DOS, then covers manipulating files and directories, using the DOS editor, printing, communicating, and finishes with a full section on batch files.

Understanding Hard Disk Management on the PC
Jonathan Kamin
500pp. Ref. 561-1

This title is a key productivity tool for all hard disk users who want efficient, error-free file management and organization. Includes details on the best ways to conserve hard disk space when using several memory-guzzling programs. Through DOS 4.

Up & Running with DR DOS 5.0
Joerg Schieb
130pp. Ref. 815-7

Enjoy a fast-paced, but thorough introduction to DR DOS 5.0. In only 20 steps, you can begin to obtain practical results: copy and delete files, password protect your data, use batch files to save time, and more.

Up & Running with DOS 3.3
Michael-Alexander Beisecker
126pp. Ref. 750-9

Learn the fundamentals of DOS 3.3 in just 20 basic steps. Each "step" is a self-contained, time-coded lesson, taking 15 minutes to an hour to complete. You learn the essentials in record time.

Up & Running with DOS 5
Alan Simpson
150pp. Ref. 774-6

A 20-step guide to the essentials of DOS 5—for busy users seeking a fast-paced overview. Steps take only minutes to complete, and each is marked with a timer clock, so you know how long each one will take. Topics include installation, the DOS Shell, Program Manager, disks, directories, utilities, customization, batch files, ports and devices, DOSKEY, memory, Windows, and BASIC.

Up & Running with Your Hard Disk
Klaus M Rubsam
140pp. Ref. 666-9

A far-sighted, compact introduction to hard disk installation and basic DOS use. Perfect for PC users who want the practical essentials in the shortest possible time. In 20 basic steps, learn to choose your hard disk, work with accessories, back up data, use DOS utilities to save time, and more.

Up & Running with Windows 286/386
Gabriele Wentges
132pp. Ref. 691-X

This handy 20-step overview gives PC users all the essentials of using Windows—whether for evaluating the software, or getting a fast start. Each self-contained lesson takes just 15 minutes to one hour to complete.

Up & Running with Windows 3.0
Gabriele Wentges
117pp. Ref. 711-8

All the essentials of Windows 3.0 in just twenty "steps"—self-contained lessons that take minutes to complete. Perfect for evaluating the software or getting a quick start with the new environment. Topics include installation, managing windows, using keyboard and mouse, using desktop utilities, and built-in programs.

Windows 3.0 Instant Reference
Marshall Moseley
195pp. Ref. 757-6

This concise, comprehensive pocket reference provides quick access to instructions on all Windows 3.0 mouse and keyboard commands. It features step-by-step instructions on using Windows, the applications that come bundled with it,

and Windows' unique help facilities. Great for all levels of expertise.

COMMUNICATIONS

Mastering Crosstalk XVI (Second Edition)
Peter W. Gofton
225pp. Ref. 642-1

Introducing the communications program Crosstalk XVI for the IBM PC. As well as providing extensive examples of command and script files for programming Crosstalk, this book includes a detailed description of how to use the program's more advanced features, such as windows, talking to mini or mainframe, customizing the keyboard and answering calls and background mode.

Mastering PROCOMM PLUS
Bob Campbell
400pp. Ref. 657-X

Learn all about communications and information retrieval as you master and use PROCOMM PLUS. Topics include choosing and using a modem; automatic dialing; using on-line services (featuring Compu-Serve), and more. Through Version 1.1b; also covers PROCOMM, the "shareware" version.

Mastering Serial Communications
Peter W. Gofton
289pp. Ref. 180-2

The software side of communications, with details on the IBM PC's serial programming, the XMODEM and Kermit protocols, non-ASCII data transfer, interrupt-level programming, and more. Sample programs in C, assembly language and BASIC.

Mastering UNIX Serial Communications
Peter W. Gofton
307pp. Ref. 708-8

The complete guide to serial communications under UNIX. Part I introduces essential concepts and techniques, while Part II explores UNIX ports, drivers, and utilities, including MAIL, UUCP, and others. Part III is for C programmers, with six in-depth chapters on communications programming under UNIX.

Up & Running with PROCOMM PLUS
Bob Campbell
134pp. Ref. 794-0
Get a fast-paced overview of telecommunications with PROCOMM PLUS, in just 20 steps. Each step takes only 15 minutes to an hour to complete, covering the essentials of installing and running the software, setting parameters, dialing, connecting with and using an online service, sending and receiving files, using macros and scripts, and operating a bulletin board.

NETWORKS

The ABC's of Local Area Networks
Michael Dortch
212pp. Ref. 664-2
This jargon-free introduction to LANs is for current and prospective users who see general information, comparative options, a look at the future, and tips for effective LANs use today. With comparisons of Token-Ring, PC Network, Novell, and others.

The ABC's of Novell NetWare
Jeff Woodward
282pp. Ref. 614-6
For users who are new to PC's or networks, this entry-level tutorial outlines each basic element and operation of Novell. The ABC's introduces computer hardware and software, DOS, network organization and security, and printing and communicating over the netware system.

Mastering Novell NetWare
Cheryl C. Currid
Craig A. Gillett
500pp. Ref. 630-8
This book is a thorough guide for System Administrators to installing and operating a microcomputer network using Novell Netware. Mastering covers actually setting up a network from start to finish, design, administration, maintenance, and troubleshooting.

UTILITIES

The Computer Virus Protection Handbook
Colin Haynes
192pp. Ref. 696-0
This book is the equivalent of an intensive emergency preparedness seminar on computer viruses. Readers learn what viruses are, how they are created, and how they infect systems. Step-by-step procedures help computer users to identify vulnerabilities, and to assess the consequences of a virus infection. Strategies on coping with viruses, as well as methods of data recovery, make this book well worth the investment.

Mastering the Norton Utilities 5
Peter Dyson
400pp, Ref. 725-8
This complete guide to installing and using the Norton Utilities 5 is a must for beginning and experienced users alike. It offers a clear, detailed description of each utility, with options, uses and examples— so users can quickly identify the programs they need and put Norton right to work. Includes valuable coverage of the newest Norton enhancements.

Mastering PC Tools Deluxe 6
For Versions 5.5 and 6.0
425pp, Ref. 700-2
An up-to-date guide to the lifesaving utilities in PC Tools Deluxe version 6.0 from installation, to high-speed back-ups, data recovery, file encryption, desktop applications, and more. Includes detailed background on DOS and hardware such as floppies, hard disks, modems and fax cards.

Mastering SideKick Plus
Gene Weisskopf
394pp. Ref. 558-1
Employ all of Sidekick's powerful and expanded features with this hands-on guide to the popular utility. Features include comprehensive and detailed coverage of time management, note taking, outlining, auto dialing, DOS file management, math, and copy-and-paste functions.

SYBEX Computer Books
are different.

Here is why . . .

At SYBEX, each book is designed with you in mind. Every manuscript is carefully selected and supervised by our editors, who are themselves computer experts. We publish the best authors, whose technical expertise is matched by an ability to write clearly and to communicate effectively. Programs are thoroughly tested for accuracy by our technical staff. Our computerized production department goes to great lengths to make sure that each book is well-designed.

In the pursuit of timeliness, SYBEX has achieved many publishing firsts. SYBEX was among the first to integrate personal computers used by authors and staff into the publishing process. SYBEX was the first to publish books on the CP/M operating system, microprocessor interfacing techniques, word processing, and many more topics.

Expertise in computers and dedication to the highest quality product have made SYBEX a world leader in computer book publishing. Translated into fourteen languages, SYBEX books have helped millions of people around the world to get the most from their computers. We hope we have helped you, too.

For a complete catalog of our publications:

SYBEX, Inc. 2021 Challenger Drive, #100, Alameda, CA 94501
Tel: (415) 523-8233/(800) 227-2346   Telex: 336311
Fax: (415) 523-2373